THE
MODERN DAY

SPARTAN

Thax Turner & Ronald "Bo" Bryant

TheModernDaySpartan.com

DEDICATION

To those with the Spartan attitude! Those who understand the importance of brain and brawn, friends and family, work and play and most importantly those authentic few who are loyal to themselves and never stop fighting for what they believe in. To those that are not afraid to believe, dream, fight and love without wavering.

To all of those before who told us we couldn't, thank you for the motivation. For all of those before us who told us we could, thanks for the mentorship and leadership!

To all of the radical thinkers who have changed the world. If not for you we would not be here.

This book is dedicated to our wives, Donna Turner and Jennifer Bryant, our biggest supporters and cheerleaders. You have continued to encourage us with all our crazy endeavors throughout the years. Thanks for your unconditional love. And to our collective children; Chance Turner who has helped me see the "best in me". Connor Turner (my bonus child) keep fighting the good fight! So proud of you both. To Emily & Asher my little mini Spartans, you keep me moving. To Uncle Les, who has always seen the potential in me and always encouraged and supported me. To our Mothers, who gave even when they had nothing but love and support. Growing up, we may have not been rich in wealth, but always rich in love. To Carolyn, thank you for your unconditional love throughout the years and being a wonderful support center. To our sisters, thank you for the love and support! And to all family, friends, and people who inspired and mentored us. Without all of you we would not exist spiritually, physically, or mentally... we are very grateful.

CONTENTS

ACKNOWLEDGMENTS

We have met a lot of Modern Day Spartans along this journey from rags to riches.

We acknowledge and deeply thank the McClelland family for embracing our Modern Day Spartan and our Intrapreneur spirit. Your vision, passion and sense of community compels us!

Jim Del Rosso, your work ethic is second to none.

Derrick Sweet, your books and insight helped shape this idea and our motivation.

David Boozer, your vision helped us bring this to the world!

Our amazing clients and colleagues; for your insights, information and knowledge. There are too many to name and for that we are blessed but we have to call out some amazing Modern Day Spartans like Darren Moore, Rodney Barton, Tommy Percell, Chris Jenkins, Dean Curtis, Merritt Powell, Evan and Antonio, and Kevin Martel... thank you for embracing our vision early, proofing our work and providing us with unbelievable feedback!

Frank Pohl, your dedication and example to life and balance.

Garrett J White, the original Modern Day Spartan!

Bill Duke, you saw my potential and took a risk.

Mike Grogan, you turned me on to expanding my horizons.

You are all Modern Day Spartans!

i

INTRODUCTION

Honor in life, Honor in death!

Most of us are aware of the Spartan Army and their amazing battles. More now than ever we are aware of the romanticized idea of the Spartans thanks to the movie 300 from director Zack Snyder. Contrary to what has been romanticized, not all Spartans were warrior elites as depicted in the movies. However for the residents of the state of Sparta in Ancient Greece during the early 2nd century B.C. all Spartans were raised with a belief and a militant mentality that was pervasive throughout the entire culture. It is important to call out that the Modern Day Spartan represents more of the ideals of the people of Sparta and not just the elite warriors that often times come to mind when we hear their name.

The people of Sparta had a code that paved the way for modern day western civilization and an ideal of democracy. These are the parallels and the stories we will draw from to introduce you to the modern day Spartan; how a culture, a "mess", and an "equal's" mentality that shaped history has brought us to revive their examples and apply them to modern day life. As one of the richest, most triumphant, balanced and fair cultures in the modern world, it is incumbent upon us to challenge how we currently view life, love, business and faith... and compare that to a time since past.

As a product of single family homes, both of us were afforded very little in the form of trappings and luxury. Like the Spartans, we came from nothing more than an ideal. We were poor from a socioeconomic standing but we were nevertheless rich in self-esteem. Both of our mothers fought hard to instill the values of integrity, faith, and the belief that we could do and be anything we wanted, regardless of what society may have expected from us.

Thax often jokes that when he was kid, whenever rent was due -- that meant it was time to move! This book is less about our hardships and what we had to endure growing up poor and underprivileged and more about the lessons and the mindset that was forged from our consequences. Amazing thing and people have become the invaluable byproduct of strife and struggle. We remember our past but we do not dwell on it. We learn from it, using it as a reminder of what we went through and how we got here. While we hold no shame about our beginnings we also never want to go back.

The motivation for this book started from a story in ancient Sparta about King Lykurgos (776 BC). As Sparta began its history some 200 plus years earlier King Lykurgos in undoubtable credited with forming what became known the architecture for a successful civilization.

As *the story goes:*

Lykurgos was the son of King Eumenos. When his father died, his older brother Polydektes became king. Shortly after becoming king, Polydektes died as well. Lykurgos succeeded his older brother and at that time, the wife of Polydektes, still pregnant with the former kings child, offered herself to Lykurgos as his new wife and queen (again). She was carrying the child of Polydektes, and as a sacrifice, she had asked Lykurgos to rid her of her unborn child after they wed. This was a very political thing and while it was acceptable for the wife of a former king to marry the new king, it was socially taboo for a king to marry a woman with another man's child, even if it was that man's unborn nephew.

Lykurgos knew his new wife was an unrelenting and ambitious woman, so he agreed to both taking her as his wife and ridding her of her child. When his nephew was born, he had agreed to "disappear the child," but instead he took the child to the Agora (village square) and proclaimed him the heir of the throne, giving him the name of Charilaos which meant "Joy of the

People." This young king, Charilaos, would be raised by the people, for the people. When his new wife found out what had happened, she was enraged and sought revenge against Lykurgos. It was too late to do anything about her child as he was now protected and untouchable, but that would not stop her form ruining and sabotaging King Lykurgos... and eventually Sparta. To avoid bloodshed and the potential chaos this would cause to Sparta, Lykurgos fled.

Lykurgos traveled to Crete, then Asia and Egypt, later we went to Spain, Libya and India. All along the way, he studied the different cultures, laws and constitutions of these various countries.

Armed with a vast knowledge and broader understanding of the world and its people, Lykurgos returned to Greece to improve Sparta and create equality. He first had to seek approval from the Oracle. He knew laws would be controversial as he planned to divide the land owned by the rich, and give it to all Spartans equally. His laws would provide accountability to every person, and they would demand that everyone contribute to Sparta regardless of wealth, status or privilege. He would persuade them to accept his new laws and views. The Oracle had deemed him "more God than man" and with this blessing, he returned to Sparta. This was a true turning point in the Spartan evolution. Upon his return, he found his nephew Charilaos was now a young man and King of Sparta. This provided Lykurgos a platform and a collaboration to help implement his new laws.

These new laws were going to be a big change for the comfortable Spartans but a necessary change nonetheless. In order to persuade the Spartans to accept his laws and the discomfort these laws would bring to some people, Lykurgos created a live model for people to see.

Lykurgos had bred and raised two dogs. One dog was a house dog with domestic comforts, food, freedom and lack of structure while the other dog was an outdoor dog bread to hunt and kill in order to live and survive. Lykurgos gathered the people around to announce the new laws and demonstrate the impact these laws would have to their culture. The demonstration successfully illustrated how his new laws would impact the people. From observing the two dogs, the Spartans understood how completely useless the untrained house dog was and that they too, as a people, had become soft and useless. The poor embraced the new laws and the rich, who had the most to lose, opposed these new laws.

At the demonstration, a youth from one of the wealthy families, named Alkander, struck Lykurgos in the eye. Lykurgos lost his eye but did not prosecute the youth. Instead he took him in as a servant and afforded him the chance to discover his character and potential. Alkander later became one of his most loyal and devoted disciples.

From his wisdom, calculation and perceived kindness, Lykurgos later won over all of the people of Sparta and his laws were finally accepted. Toward the end of his successful reign as King, Sparta flourished. The balance and the harmony of the city was that of a truly utopian society. Adored and loved by his people and upon his decline, Lykurgos decided to leave Sparta. In a farewell speech to the Spartans, he had asked that none of his laws be changed until his return. Honor being what it was in Sparta, the people agreed and Lykurgos left.

Later in Delphi, knowing he would soon die, he made it a point to never physically be able to return to Sparta in any form and order to ensure the laws would be honored and never changed he ordered his body burned and his ashes spread throughout the land in Crete.

When we first heard this story, we both identified with the hunting dog and the moral of the story. The impact of equality and the idea that your circumstance should not define you but instead you should be able to define yourself. Start from a clean slate, and make your mark upon this world, understanding that you have to be hungry, you have to be uncomfortable at times, you have to contribute, and most importantly, you have to be accountable.

Like this story, many of the lessons we will be covering will engage your mind and maybe even make you feel a little uncomfortable. While certainly by today's standards, some of the cultural practices of the Spartans may be taboo, we still stand to learn, and can apply these core values to the way we live and think today.

Spartans stood for a great number of things and were devout to their cause above all else. They were much more than a warring culture. They were a community of farmers and poets, artists and thinkers. In the next chapter, we will highlight the parallels from Sparta and apply them to practical, real life examples in your personal, professional and spiritual life.

Lastly, we encourage you to use this as a workbook. Highlight the parts that speak to you, dog ear the pages you need to remember, and make notes to expand upon your thoughts and practices. As we like to say... "Get dirty" and

"LIVE YOUR LIFE ON PURPOSE!"

Throughout the book you will find helpful little facts, quotes and motivations as indicated by the following key.

 The helmet represents the brain or clarity in thinking. When you see this symbol we will be illustrating the thinking part of the battle plan.

 The Spears represent strategic thinking. When you see this symbol we will be illustrating the strategic part of the battle plan.

 The Shield represents defensive thinking. When you see this symbol we will be illustrating protection strategy.

 The Winged Shoes represent the path. When you see this symbol we will be illustrating the path of the Modern Day Spartan.

 The Sword represents the offensive path. When you see this symbol we will be illustrating the tactical thoughts embraced of the way of the Modern Day Spartan.

PART 1

THE MODERN DAY SPARTAN

"THE PATH"

THE SPARTAN MINDSET

Why the Modern Day Spartan? Because life is a balance of war, art, family and community! The Modern Day Spartan has to be strategic in their thinking, inventive in their ideas, inclusive in their plans and balanced in their life. Not all of your ideas will be embraced nor will your thinking. The Modern Day Spartan is on a mission to create a healthy and active lifestyle full of balance as you strive to bring out the best in yourself and the people around you. The MDS is fearless and persistent in everything they touch.

A Spartan is "Noble in Life, Noble in death".

To be a modern day Spartan you must first adopt the mindset. There is no tool, no advice, and no idea that can ever be fully realized until you have adopted the proper mindset. You must clear the confusion of what people or society tell you to be and focus instead upon who you truly are and strive to be that best version of yourself.

"A confused mind does nothing".
~ Unknown

The Spartans lived by a code and so must we. The Spartan code stood for a purpose larger than ourselves as an individual. Self-sacrifice for the greater good was the key cornerstone in the Spartan's way of life. While this was both a figurative and literal belief to the Spartans, the Modern Day Spartan applies this belief in all facets of their life. At home a modern day Spartan gives as much of themselves as they take from others. At work the modern day Spartan will put aside a selfish goal for the betterment of the organization. In faith they will know no shame and put charity in front of their wants and desires. In health, they will take great care to be an example for their children and their social circles.

 "A Spartan will not engage in a path or a cause that is not noble. Life, Faith, Health and Business require a conviction and passion in order to truly walk this path. A Spartan is authentic and true to themselves."
~ Ron Bryant

The Spartans scorned wealth and luxury. We interpret that today to mean that a modern day Spartan cannot be governed by the trappings of money and material possessions. That is not to say that you should live modestly and not enjoy these material things but more that you must work for a greater cause and have deeper desire along your path than to be ruled by money and things.

Spartans were not grandiose in their own affairs. Spartans did not believe in telling their own stories or engaging in shameless acts of self-promotion. To apply that to today, we must let others do the bragging about us. We can all become legends through our actions and from the remarkable actions being witnessed and told by others. We must plant seed and be thoughtful. After all the word Sparta translates from the verb "I sow" or 'To sow".

Spartan culture was one of the first cultures on record to live with democratic thinking. When the soldiers were away, the women ran the state and its affairs. Women were free to express their opinions in public, to drink, to think and even to pick their own suitor. The Spartan culture was one of great equality. Everyone had a role and every role in their society was a valued one because the society would not run without a single member and the role would not be fulfilled.

While some of this language and these ideas may seem like a no brainer, this was not the conventional wisdom of the time. The Spartan culture was a fair and equal culture and very progressive in their societal views. We draw an equal lesson as a Modern Day Spartan. If you think about it, not that much has changed. The modern day Spartan treats everyone as equals. Regardless of the paths we cross we are no better than anyone we could possibly judge so we should not judge at all. There is no equal or greater in the mind of an MDS; be it socioeconomic, gender, race, creed, religion or affiliation. We are no better than anyone and stand to learn from everyone!

 "If you are the smartest person in the room, you are in the wrong room".

In Sparta, the cities were not protected by great walls and defenses. These cities were defended by their people instead or mortal and brick. By the men and women of the community. Some fought, some governed, some supported the fighters and others were tactical in the development of battle plans. The modern lesson we can draw from the Spartan's way of defending their cities is more metaphorical than it is literal. First and most important, the Spartans understood the value of team, collaboration and contribution. Spartans did not put up walls. They had confidence in themselves and in their community to be open, transparent and approachable. This is the real lesson of the MDS. We must be honest, open and vulnerable. We must not put up walls to protect ourselves because when we do, we close others out and miss our opportunities for teamwork, collaboration and contributing for the greater good. This authenticity and being comfortable with yourself is paramount above all else when starting the path of the Modern Day Spartan. In order to truly be authentic and in order to be a Modern Day Spartan you must always strive to be the best, most authentic you and constantly strive for improvement.

The Spartan culture lived by a principle to be "perfectly human". That is of course an oxymoron but that was its intent. The Spartans understood: **"to be human is to error"** but in correcting those errors and learning from their mistakes they were always in a state of progression. Self-progression! The modern day lesson is exactly the same for the MDS. We have an expression we use called failing forward. The idea of failing forward is the idea that we encourage failure. We also understand that people don't fail, things fail. Failure is attached to a person and if you never give up and never relent you may fail but you will never be a failure. Fail well my friends!

Thax's grandmother had a great perspective on failure.

She said, "Thax, never let failure stop you; failure is just a measure of how badly a person desires something. If you just 'think' that you want to achieve a goal, the very first obstacle encountered will generally be enough to make you want to give up in despair and say, 'well, I guess that it just wasn't meant for me.' However, if you truly desire something, you keep going until you have successfully completed your mission."

This mentality ties in to one of our favorite quotes from Henry Ford.

 "Whether you think you can or you think you can't, you're probably right."

Spartans were also known for their discipline. They were relentless in their pursuit for training, understanding and development. They used their brains as much as they used their brawn.

A healthy male Spartan child was chosen at birth to be a great warrior. They were bathed in wine when they were born to rid them of any evil. They were not coddled in order to make them independent and self-reliant. They were left in isolation in order to develop their sense of self and independence. They were captive in the dark for extended amounts of time to teach them not to fear the dark and also to help them develop their other senses. While today some of their ways seemed harsh they were meaningful training techniques in a time of war and for survival. They intentionally leaned into the discomfort in order to better themselves.

A warrior child was often deprived of food so that they could appreciate the value of food. A starving warrior child was taught to steal food in order to survive. This sharpened their survival instincts. What's more, if that child was caught stealing food they would be beaten twice. Once by the landowner or farmer that they stole from and again from their instructor for getting caught. The idea was to make them think, strategize and be resourceful instead of desperate. To teach them how to live off the land instead of depending on others. Not to react but to think and plan and prepare.

To be clear, we are not advocating that you starve, steal, and/or deprive yourself or others of basic human needs but the real lesson to draw from the logic of the Spartan culture is that in order to truly appreciate having something you need to know what it is to go without. This can be applied in so many of our day to day disciplines and in some cases the translation can be taken literally. Many cultures still practice fasting to know hunger so that they can appreciate a full belly. One of the things that drew us together to write this book and share our message was our similar background and upbringing. We were both the byproduct of a single family home below or right at the poverty line and while not as severe we were both deprived and had to learn how to live off the land, be resourceful and self-reliant. "Those lessons made us who we are. Our success is owed to these moments. It has kept us grateful, disciplined and sharp".

We know these lessons will not just propel us forward and motivate us in the form of fear. (The fear that moves you forward as to not go backwards). These lessons should also teach us to continually practice this discomfort in order to keep ourselves grounded, mindful and sharp in our faculties.

 I have learned over the years that when one's mind is made up, this diminishes fear; knowing what must be done does away with fear.
~ Rosa Parks

The Spartans were more mindful of the human condition than any other culture in history. They understood that people were more motivated by fear than they were by success. Spartans understood that change and discomfort were common elements that people avoided. They also understood how people thought when it came to strategy. They knew that the last thing an enemy would expect from them was likely the first thing that they would do. The more radical the idea, the more inclined they were to employ it as a tactic or as part of their overall strategy. In these lessons time has changed nothing. The Modern Day Spartan will use all of these tactics and strategies as well.

 "The path less taken has yet to be stripped of its riches".
~ Unknown

Spartans also understood the art of aggression but more importantly the art of retreat. In a great battle against the Persian Army, after defeating a large faction of the infantry came the legendary battle of the Spartan's 300. Where 300 warriors held off Zurkzees Persian army of over 200,000. In this battle, the Spartans did the unthinkable, they retreated. This was after two days of holding off the 200,000 and decimating a large portion of the infantry. At this point in the battle Zurkzees had sent in his elite forces called "the Immortals". The Immortals were rumored to be the fiercest group of fighters in the world. Thinking they had achieved victory, the Persian's Immortals gave chase to the retreating Spartans only to find they had been trapped in a tight place and surrounded by a smarter group of fighters in the Spartan army. The immortals were anything but and in short order the Spartans had obliterated this group of elite fighters while taking only minimal casualties. The lesson to draw from this retreat strategy is one of both pride and picking your battles.

The Modern Day Spartan understands that no matter how firm their beliefs and defending their views and the views of their team, not every mountain is the mountain worth dying on. Sometimes retreat can be the best offense.

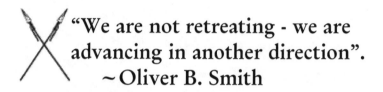 **"We are not retreating - we are advancing in another direction".**
~ Oliver B. Smith

The Spartans did have one fear but this fear was manifested intentionally. From birth Spartans are taught to fear shame. The shame of being labeled a coward, of letting down your brothers and sisters. This was the greatest fear of any Spartan and it was deeply ingrained. In the battle of the now famous 300 there were actually 301 Spartan warriors (I guess 300 sounded better). What is untold is the story of the 2 that survived. One of two took his life, the other, a great warrior named Aristadimus returned to Sparta. Upon his return he was shamed, dishonored and lost his rank as a Spartan warrior. No Spartan would afford him food or shelter or support of any kind. That is how seriously they took shame. Imagine if we were as hard on ourselves about shame as the ancient Spartans? In a day when many a moral compass doesn't point north, let this be the reminder or motivation to live with honor. Do not say a thing that you wouldn't be willing to say or do in front of your children or that you would not want to hear or see them repeat.

A Modern Day Spartan is not a coward and they do not engage in gossip or talk behind somebody's back. They address their issues immediately and directly. They fear shame but do not confuse shame with humility.

 "Cowards die many times before their deaths; the valiant never taste of death but once."
~ **Julius Caesar**

The Power of Comedy

When the odds were overwhelming or a great task was in front of them, the Spartans often handled such adversity with humor. It is said that in the Battle of Thermopylae, when the Spartans were told of the size of Xerxes army and that the number of Persians, who with their arrows could block out the sun, one Spartan's reply was "So much the better, we shall fight in the shade."

This was an early lesson I learned in my professional career from a great group that mentored me along my path. I met up with a funky band of misfits, artists and masters of their craft. I remember when I first started working with them that they were having too much fun, joking around and as my father would have said, "Playing grab ass!" Even still these guys were amazing at what they did and adored by their following... and their following was large. One day I brought up the query and I was met with a beautiful response. "Look we take what we do very seriously but that doesn't mean we have to take ourselves seriously." From that point forward I adopted the motto!

The most important thing worth fighting for! To the Spartans this was simple, friends, family and their way of life. Outside of the commonly known battle with the Persians, the Spartans were more notably always fighting with the Greeks. Yes, they too were Greek but they were Spartans first and foremost. Their biggest foe was most notably the Athenians. The two lifestyles couldn't be more opposing. The Athenians were great thinkers and consumed by wealth and status while the Spartans only fought to protect their pursuit of the perfect life surrounded by family and friends and defending anyone who would impose upon their tradition with a furious vengeance unlike anything the world has ever seen. You may have met someone like this in your life, either personally or professionally. They are a Modern Day Spartan and if you were anything like me when you met them you were in awe of how authentic they were and how well protected and comfortable they were and how well received they were by their peers. I have known four great people like this throughout my entire life and today they exist amongst my tightest inner circle. My mess.

 "Happiness is only real when it is shared."
~ Eli Neri

Honor is the byproduct of uncertainty. The Spartans understood this concept above anything else. In ancient battles to engage in a mortal combat was something of an honor. You were hand to hand against an opponent and the outcome was certain but the victor was not. Someone would die but the playing field was even. Hand to hand, sword to sword, spear to spear. Nobody had an advantage in a weapon so with the battle being even, the only certainty was that one of you was going to die and approaching a fight without anything in your favor was the purest version of honor to a Spartan. These lessons are not as easy to find today. Honor in modern terms exists in standing up for what is right, saying what is necessarily even when it is unpopular. The Modern Day Spartan understands the honor in uncertainty.

 "Integrity is not doing the right thing when people are looking but rather doing the right thing when they are not."

The Spartan's life was always in motion. In both their lives and at war the Spartans understood the need for both teamwork and agility. Often times the army would break away from the core group and go into groups of 12. The progression of a Spartan warrior from training to becoming a warrior meant you would graduate into a "Mess". This was your group of 12 that you ate with, slept with, and fought with. You always had each other's back. In war and in life the entirety of Sparta was a group but the sub-layer of that group was the Mess. The Mess was shoulder to shoulder on the battle field and they always fought together because they understood the power of having each other's back and always knowing where their Mess was. While other armies of the period had to walk in lock step and charge head on, the Spartans would break into their respective Mess and come at their enemy from all angles. They were fluid instead of rigid, mobile instead of slow, effective instead of formed.

"Once your mindset changes, everything on the outside will change along with it."

THE SPARTAN'S MANTRA

Selflessness

Perseverance

Adventurous

Relentless

Tenacious

Analytical

Nimble

Spiritual

This mantra is more than a list of words to the Modern Day Spartan. These are the adjectives that describe and define us. A Modern Day Spartan is not an idea but a way of life. We strive to improve everyday by living our mantra.

The lack of cowardice in the Spartan's way of life also provides a modern day lesson. While other armies would hide behind camouflage the Spartans stood out in the open proudly wearing their crimson color, never afraid to be seen and never afraid of conflict. When an opposing army would scout the Spartans to see their numbers and weapons so that they could report back to camp, the Spartans would not acknowledge the scout nor would they give chase. They were calm, cool and otherwise not distracted. Just like the young Spartan that had to steal food, they had learned through discipline that calm thinking and planning would win out the day. The modern day human condition has softened many of us and many people today in life do hide behind a camouflage. We react to how people think we should be instead of holding true to who we really are. They are afraid to show their true self. Afraid of conflict. Afraid to wear their colors with pride. Pride of family, pride of spirituality, pride of their beliefs. A Modern Day Spartan is authentic and transparent to all that shall cross their path.

THE SPARTAN'S CREED

The Spartan is on a quest for freedom. Freedom of money, freedom of time and freedom of purpose.
The Spartan is not selfish with their ideas; when they learn, they share.
A Spartan understands the value of collaboration and is not interested in making themselves stronger without making the entire team stronger.
A Spartan finds likeminded people that fight for faith, family and purpose.
In a world where ideals have become unpopular the Spartan will win out the day.
The Spartan will pick their battles wisely and know what mountains are worth dying on.
The Spartan understands sacrifice and knows we occasionally have to lose the battle to win the war.
We are balanced, deliberate and authentic.
There is not one of us amongst the best of us better than the rest of us.

THE MODERN DAY SPARTAN

Extraction

From this path, the learning and stories of Sparta we have extracted a path we call the...

Spartan's Eco-system

We focus on four cornerstones in the path to becoming a "Modern Day Spartan".

- **Success**
- **Balance**
- **Power**
- **Lifestyle**

Success is a measure of more things than just money. We all measure it differently but whatever it looks like to you it is important you hold that close. Success in Sparta was measured by their faith in each other, their culture, their friends and family and above all preserving their way of life.

Balance is in work and life and finding the harmony between the two. In life specifically you must have balance in faith, family, friends, finance and fitness. We measure the balance of Sparta and the Utopia they created with this principle.

Power is not ego or the idea of being in control. It is quite the opposite. Control is an illusion, the

only thing we can control in life is ourselves and
our actions. What we do, say, believe and become
is all within our control... nothing more, nothing
less. Personal power comes from letting go of
control or the illusion of control and focusing soley
on that in which you can control. You! That is
lesson. Letting go creates great empowerment and
sets you on a path for personal development. The
Spartans understood this above all else. This was at
their core.

Lifestyle is personal and subjective. Being the best
version of yourself, striving for balance and success
and achieving your personal power are all essential
parts of the equation.

Here is where the momentum shifts. These are not
competing ideas. These ideals have to be managed
in tandem.

Trust me, this is easier said than done. We have all
been there. Given our past and where we came
from, we both suffered for many years with a life
out of balance. Coming from poverty we put the
rest of our lives out of balance to push for success
because we knew we never wanted to back to where
we came from. It wasn't until we both embraces
and practiced this formula that our true success
really manifested itself.

Here is the take away and the implementation plan

to capturing your path to becoming a Modern Day Spartan.

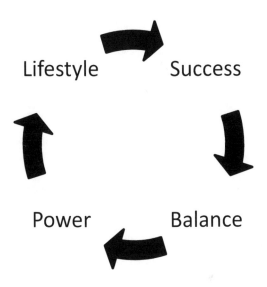

Lifestyle → Success → Balance → Power → (Lifestyle)

Understand the outline above is not built to become 4 competing ideas. It is instead an Ecosystem and when one piece of the Ecosystem gets interrupted we cannot achieve optimum output or outcome.

If you can identify with us and you know what it is to be out of balance, always trying to catch up, overcompensating when something gets out of whack... then this formula will have a great impact on you and those around you.

If you have ever focused too much on one thing

only to have that create fires in other areas of your life from the things you ignored and you constantly feel like you are being pulled in every direction... then this formula is for you.

If you have ever thought to yourself, "There has to be a better way."... then this is the formula for you.

Here is the illustration of the Ecosystem.

THE HEALTHY SPARTAN

"Do you not know that you are God's temple and that god's Sprit dwells in you?" ~ *1 corinthians 3:16*

In Spartan history there is much little talked about outside of the epic and well known battles that have drawn the attention of Hollywood and folklore. Most people are unaware of the fact that it was the Spartan architecture that is responsible for building the famous Greek temple, the brazen house of Athena. Another overlooked fact about Spartan culture lies in the balance the early Spartan's had. They were a group of farmers, artisans, great poets and even Olympians. From 720 BC to 576 BC, out of 81 Olympic victors Sparta had 46 of them. To have more than half of the winners come from just one city-state out of the total number of cities that participated was unheard of.

These accomplishments were made possible for many reasons ranging from the support of their community, the teamwork throughout Sparta and most importantly because of the Spartan discipline. Spartans undoubtedly were born and raised with an iron constitution and an expectation of pride, honor and discipline. As Modern Day Spartans we need to draw from these early examples so that we too can succeed beyond expectation.

As Modern Day Spartans we understand the importance of health. A healthy body and healthy mind in concert will create an untouchable ecosystem that will provide us with endurance, stamina, longevity, clarity and focus.

As a rule, we must focus on our body for it is the temple that houses our brain and as our most important asset we must protect it and be just as disciplined as the Spartan's of the past.

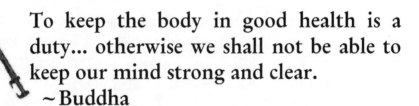 **To keep the body in good health is a duty... otherwise we shall not be able to keep our mind strong and clear.**
  ~ Buddha

Balance is the easiest thing to give up. We can quit through many forms of rationalization. If you are like many people you have battled with some form of balance. Be it your health, your weight, your education, your spirituality, etc. Whatever the case may be we end up giving up on something when it becomes too hard or it begins to interfere with our comfort or quality of life. What we know for sure is that if you continue to attack a problem the same way and continue to fail it is not because you have failed to identify the problem accurately but rather that you have failed to remedy the problem appropriately. For many people that have an unhealthy relationship with diet and exercise it is not for lack of identifying the problem but rather in how you attack it. When we are overweight due to poor diet or lack of exercise we tend to reach a point of frustration and then we attack the problem. The problem is how we attack these issues. It is not uncommon for us to start an exercise routine or diet regimen that is both impractical and extreme. They are usually so extreme in fact, that they usually are doomed to fail from the beginning.

The modern Day Spartan understands balance and it is balance that is required to attack this and every other goal you have when it comes to accomplishing your balanced life. You must attack your challenges in a balanced way. That is to say you must have a measurable, realistic approach to the problem. As it is said, "Rome was not built in a day". Looking at any challenge in your life you must understand that it didn't take a day, a week or even a month to get you into the current situation you are trying to change so to it will not be remedied that quickly either. When approaching a balanced, sustainable path to good health, you must attack the problem in a way that is sustainable. From the beginning, after formulating your plan, ask yourself if this is something that you will be able to incorporate into your life for the rest of your life?

You do not have to work out for 2 hours a day, 5 days a week. Likely that will create imbalance somewhere else in your life and again it would not be sustainable. However, if you are not working out at all or very little, how hard would it be to do just 15 to 20 minutes of high intensity exercise 5 days a week? Likely this would be a more sustainable path and while the results may not happen as quickly they will eventually come to fruition and have a greater chance of helping you achieve sustainability.

Our relationship with food is no different. Extreme diets can have an amazing impact and can help us achieve great results. However, this too can be an ill-fated plan. How sustainable is the extreme diet? Can you approach your diet in a healthy sustainable way? Can you eat better throughout the week and afford yourself some indulgence on the weekend instead? Can you minimize your portions or modify just one bad habit at a time? Again, the key is modify not eliminate. Eliminating things in your diet will most likely cause eventual failure but instead of indulging everyday can you make your indulgence a reward at the end of the week? Minor adjustments in both your diet and your exercise routine will eventually put you on a path to success. Balance and moderation are the keys to this successful battle plan and your eventual path to becoming a healthy Modern Day Spartan.

We all know what needs to be done, we usually fail in the how. Fail forward and keep trying. Review, rework and revise your plan and keep moving forward. This is the Modern Day Spartans path!

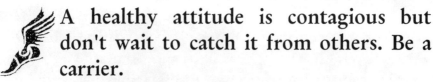 **A healthy attitude is contagious but don't wait to catch it from others. Be a carrier.**
   ~ Tom Stoppard

DEFINE YOUR LIFE

Any successful warrior lives by a set of their own rules. This is not to say that they do not follow rules but instead they define personal rules for themselves. Akin with the Spartans from the past they have discipline and courage to be themselves. They have personal integrity in what they do, how they deal with people, situations and their emotions. These are not rules that can be told to you but instead rules you already know you should be living by.

Here is courage, mankind's finest possession, here is
the noblest prize that a young man can endeavor to win,
and it is a good thing his city and all the people share with
him when a man plants his feet and stands in the foremost
spears relentlessly, all thought of foul flight completely
forgotten,
and has well trained his heart to be steadfast and to endure,
and with words encourages the man who is stationed beside
him.
Here is a man who proves himself to be valiant in war...

(Translation by Richmond Lattimore, from the book "Greek Lyrics," University of Chicago Press, 1960)

Engagement was another rule of the Spartan and yet again a parallel to draw into modern day life. The opposition will tend to show you an opening that you can't help but take. Do not be fooled as these are nothing different than a modern day Trojan horse. I know we are mixing our metaphors but there is no Trojan horse in the Spartan record because they didn't bite on such things... because they had their rules.

Most people spend much wasted time in their life trying to get people to see them favorably. Working too hard to impress others. Bending to the interpretation we think others want to see from us. A Modern Day Spartan has a firm conviction of self and would only worry about what someone thinks of them if they were to compromise themselves and have that be revealed.

True success in life comes from this definition. The most successful cases of a balanced life teach us this discipline in the following 7 examples:

- **Discipline in Schedule.**
- **Structure and Organization.**
- **Balance of Work, Family and Friends.**
- **Dedication to Self Improvement.**
- **Seeking feedback in all forms.**
- **Practice of the Golden Rule.**
- **Philanthropy.**

THE MODERN DAY SPARTAN

DISCIPLINE IN SCHEDULE

The best of the best have a routine as it relates to their schedule. They know how to perform at their best and most certainly what underperformance looks like and moreover what it is caused by. Unhealthy sleeping, eating and exercise habits will not leave you at your best. The Spartans were machines. Their commitment to being fit and healthy in body mind, spirit and balance was not what they did to be successful but rather their success was found because of it.

STRUCTURE AND ORGANIZATION

The Modern Day Spartan understands the need for structure and organization. The work they do, the life they live and the people they touch are impacted because of this. By organizing your thoughts, actions and surroundings your outcomes will be better because of it. The Spartans knew how to plan their work and work their plan. When we have a map we are more likely to get where we are going.

BALANCE OF SELF, FAMILY, FRIENDS AND WORK

This is the most important element of the seven! In understanding balance you must look at it as a goal; not one to achieve but one to constantly strive for. The reason it is so hard to accomplish is because we always tend to react to the need instead of create the rules. The proactive approach to a balanced life goes immediately back to discipline in schedule, structure and organization. Creating a stop and start time for this balance is the best way to achieve it. Creating tradition around all of these events that are made aware to others will create both respect and expectation of this balance.

DEDICATION TO SELF IMPROVEMENT

Much like balance, improvement is not something with an ending point. It is constant. In order to be able to manage this you must first let go of the illusion of control. It has been said before but if you are the smartest person in the room, you are in the wrong room. Self-improvement is organic but intentional. Much like any organic item when it stops growing it starts dying. This applies to your brain as much as your brawn.

A Modern Day Spartan will seek discomfort. In order to grow we have to get outside of our comfort zone. The easiest way to initiate the path to improvement is recognition of both your literal and figurative strengths and your weaknesses. Identify your passions and your interests and expand upon them. Find the things you avoid and lean into the discomfort.

SEEKING FEEDBACK IN ALL FORMS

As human beings we struggle with this one the most. Ego rules us and we fear criticism. That is what holds us back from true growth. The hardest things to hear are the things we fear. They are usually of no surprise but the chemical precursor that is initiated at the sound of criticism renders the logical side of the brain from being able to participate, absorb and reflect. Instead we usually deflect, react and rationalize. Reading the process should create a level of understanding. Even when you think someone could be wrong, the message should still be internalized for at a minimum you will at least be able to understand the perception you give someone, real or otherwise. Gravitate away from those who promote you and seek out those who make you feel vulnerable. Know the difference and use this to develop yourself instead of diminish yourself.

PRACTICE OF THE GOLDEN RULE

This too has been covered but it bears repeating. Use empathy as a tool. We do not mistake kindness for weakness yet we draw the lessons needed in life to understand that any given situation could be or has been our situation. Never losing sight of where we came from will allow us to get where we are intending to go. There is no judgment to be ashamed of when it comes to doing the right thing.

PHILANTHROPY

Giving back comes in many forms. A Modern Day Spartan will immediately practice the form in which they were given. When you are struggling to find out where to focus your charity, think back to where it was given to you. A Spartan understands the importance of the hand up versus the hand out. For as we improve it is only fair that we should expect the same from others. Do be careful not to allow that line to get blurred otherwise it will turn into judgment and that is not what a Modern Day Spartan will engage in. Judgment will only create weakness and vulnerability. If you feel like you have never been given a thing then let that be the reason you give. Philanthropy can exist in the simplest of forms but know this... standing for nothing greater than self does not allow greatness for anyone including you.

THE BATTLEFIELD OF THE MIND

Our minds are a battleground for our wills. Good struggles against evil. Our values fluctuate between what we want — immediate gratification — and what we know is better for us.

At the peak of its power an incredible series of events and mishaps led to the fall of Sparta from being the dominant power in the Aegean to becoming a second rate army.

Shortly after their victory of Greece, the Spartans turned against their Persian backers that helped them take Greece and attached Turkey. The Spartan army eventually became fragmented and they were forced to campaign on several fronts.

The Spartan's had become jaded. They had built wall to keep their enemies out. They fought to advance instead of protect and eventually they had lost sight of what they stood for. Inevitably their ego and their greed overtook their beliefs and their faith. The war they lost was not on the battle field but instead in their minds.

WANTS VERSUS NEEDS

We are torn between what we want to do and what our conscience tells us is the right thing to do for ourselves or for society.

All great leaders struggled over wants and needs. They were torn between pleasing the electors and giving the country what was the best long-range solution—albeit a less popular one.

Not surprisingly, we've become a society that demands instant gratification. We are neither a patient nor a persistent group. We demand quick painless fixes to our problems and we want them yesterday.

 There are only two tragedies in life: one is not getting what one wants, and the other is getting it.
~ Oscar Wilde

CHOOSING THE PATH OF LEAST RESISTANCE

Unfortunately, we often choose the path more traveled because it seems safer, or easier, or more popular. If we can make no sense of a course of action, we most often avoid it.

If a course of action is potentially; physically, mentally, emotionally or socially uncomfortable, we opt to avoid it. This is one of the most basic human instincts: pleasure over pain.

 No one saves us but ourselves. No one can and no one may. We ourselves must walk the path.
~ Buddha

STUCK IN THE SELF-PITY

It is easy for us to bemoan what was and let it freeze us in place. The self-pity trap is often an excuse or a reason to let our circumstances define us...

- I grew up in a poor neighborhood. No one ever amounts to anything except a drug lord or a teenage mom in my neighborhood. How can I expect to escape this environment?

- My family never graduated from high school. Who am I to consider becoming a chemical engineer?

- I don't come from a rich family. There's no money to send me to university.

- My family doesn't even know what a neurosurgeon does. I'll get no support from them when I say I want to go to medical school.

- My family needs the money I will earn by quitting

school and going to work.

- My boss hates my family so he picks on me.

- I have a learning disability. Everyone is shocked I got this far.

- All my friends quit school. There's no incentive for me to continue.

- My employer's expectations were completely unrealistic.

If we want to find an excuse for quitting school, aborting our mission, giving up on our dream, there will always be lots of available cop outs.

 "Our past may explain why we're suffering but we must not use it as an excuse to stay in bondage,"
~ Joyce Meyer

HAVING A NEGATIVE OUTLOOK

Henry Ford noted that people are about as happy as they choose to be. If you are constantly dwelling on the negatives in life, you'll see little to attain, to dream of achieving, to wish for. It is impossible to have a positive life and a negative mind.

If you want to be happy, successful, accomplished, then you need to program that mind of yours to see the glass half full, not half empty. Better yet, you need to see the half empty glass as a challenge to fill up! This is the mentality of the Modern Day Spartan!

> "When someone tells me "no," it doesn't mean I can't do it, it simply means I can't do it with them."
> ~ Karen E. Quinones Miller

LACK OF FAITH IN YOURSELF AND OTHERS

Joyce Meyer, in Battlefield of the Mind writes, "Trust and faith bring joy to life and help relationships grow to their maximum potential." As humans, we are the least trusting of all earth's creatures. We expect that everyone has a hidden agenda. We're convinced that life is out to get us and that those in authority are gunning for us to fall flat on our faces. We seldom even trust our own intuition.

If we all learned to trust in ourselves, each other and a higher power, whatever or whomever we believed in, our world would be a happier, more peaceful place and we within it would be more self-confident, more caring and sharing of one another. Too many of us believe it's a jungle out there, and only the strongest survive. Imagine how much better your life would be if you broke the shackles of limitation bestowed upon you by your circumstances. We have witnessed it in everyday life by the people that surround us... Those that believe good will come to them, live in this same kind of place and by virtue of where you live you then become. The opposite is true in the inverse. A bad place creates bad circumstances but that place is limited within the space between your ears. Let it be said that being good for you doesn't always mean being good to you. Sometimes you will have to take the medicine that doesn't taste good but the outcome is still favorable. If the people, environment and circumstances surrounding you are defining you then you have no choice but to change your landscape. This is easier said than done and we speak as an authority on this particular form of prescription as we have both been there. We have been destined for failure and we overcame our circumstances by choice. This is the first step in the Spartan Path to overcoming the battle field of the mind!

 Doubt is a pain too lonely to know that faith is his twin brother.
~ Khalil Gibran

CONFUSING SUSPICION FOR DISCERNMENT

Along with a lack of faith in ourselves, our colleagues, the world, and a higher power, we also lack trust. We tell ourselves we are merely being discerning individuals. Joyce Meyer notes: "Some people think they have discernment when actually they are just suspicious."

In reality we are suspicious of everyone and everything. We don't trust our family, our friends, and our colleagues. We don't even trust our own judgment.

Suspicion comes out of the closed mind; discernment comes out of the renewed spirit. We fail to trust anyone including our own instincts. Instead of being introspective and believing that others have our best interests at heart, we go around second guessing   everything everybody does and says. This means we are stressed, on high alert for land mines, and completely skeptical of situations at all times. We are judgmental by nature and that is a natural byproduct of human evolution. The innate ability to judge surroundings, people and situations has kept the human race from going extinct. This is a prefrontal cortex mechanism as instinctual as eating and breathing. It is hardwired in our DNA but we must be conscious of it and understand how this can both help us and hurt us at the same time.

These suspicions can affect the way we view faith in ourselves, one another, and even a higher power.

 Suspicion always haunts the guilty mind.
~ William Shakespeare

RESISTANCE TO CHANGE

Our minds cling to what is known and what is comfortable. The human condition again states that we are more compelled by fear than we are by desire. Without being nudged we prefer to stay in that familiar realm. However, failure to grow results in stagnation or status quo. We must caution that no matter how much we know any given thing that there will always be something new to learn, something we knew that we need to be refreshed in and something we thought we knew that turned out to be wrong.

Failure to continue to grow and learn new information and new techniques will result in antiquated methods. This was the fatal flaw in the Spartan mentality and to which they eventually fell. We too will fail to remain competitive as Modern Day Spartans in business, in life and in faith if we do not learn from this peril of the mind.

The only way to make sense out of change is to plunge into it, move with it, and join the dance.
~ Alan Watts

OVERTHINKING THINGS

You can live in the mind but you have to have to trust your instincts.

Too often we think we know more than others. We overthink our responses. We overthink other's motives. We need to learn to trust our gut instincts and believe in the basic human goodness. Finally we have to trust a higher power and believe that there is a divine order to things.

We cannot solve our problems with the same thinking we used when we created them.
~ Albert Einstein

FAILURE TO TAKE RESPONSIBILITY

Convincing ourselves that whatever happens, whatever obstacle we face is someone else's fault is failing to own our problems. The path to intellectual freedom begins when we are accountable to ourselves without making excuses.

If we don't own our problems we don't feel empowered to come up with solutions either. Instead we adopt a discouraged, self-defeating attitude. This is not the road to success. This is not the attitude of a Modern Day Spartan Intrapreneur. We are allowing our mind to defeat itself.

You cannot escape the responsibility of tomorrow by evading it today.
- Abraham Lincoln

BEING IN A STATE OF STRESS AND TURMOIL

Because we do not have a feeling of self-confidence, we do not trust in our fellow man or have faith in a higher power, our minds are in turmoil. Having nothing to use as an anchor means we drift in mental uncertainty. Mental clarity and a peaceful mind from knowing your authentic self will lead you to the path of enlightenment and fulfillment. As the prophet Isaiah tells us, when the mind is stayed on the right things, it will be at rest.

TAKE THE OATH

As a Modern Day Spartan you must take an oath to venture outside of your comfort level. Identify what you gravitate away from, identify what you know to be healthy, look at those that you look up to and identify what they do differently. Once you have identified these things, explore them. We often call this "leaning into the discomfort". Whether you think you will like something or not, it is best to prove yourself right or wrong and remove all doubt. Regardless of trying new things and enjoying them or not, pleasure is less important an outcome than doing what is good for you. It is often only the destination we pay attention to when in reality all of the learning comes from the journey.

 If we are facing in the right direction, all we have to do is keep on walking.
~ Proverb

THE ART OF SURRENDER

Surrender literally means to stop fighting. Stop fighting with yourself and others. Stop resisting and pushing against reality; stop fighting the governing laws of the universe and the natural flow of things.

The fine art of surrender is a skill and a gift. The art of surrender calls us to release what we might think is the best way of doing something so that we can open to a more truly inspired way. Surrender is when we let go of swimming upstream and learn to go with the flow of life. We learn to surrender what we think people want us to be and find our authentic self. We surrender limited thinking and small visions in order to see a bigger picture. Sometimes when we surrender we stop fighting and through the clear mind we are able to see through our fights and our battles that we once held so dear. We are open to new ideas, inspiration and grace.

Everybody wants happiness, nobody wants pain, but you can't have a rainbow without a little rain.
~ Unknown

Remember the battle of Thermopylae and how the Spartans retreated. They did so in order to gain a more favorable position and what looked like surrender turned into advantage.

- **What do you fear?**

- **What holds you back?**

- **What do you want?**

- **Why aren't you better?**

- **Why aren't you stronger?**

- **Why aren't you smarter?**

There is so much more you are capable of, yet you linger here, weak and afraid. You know what you want, whether you realize it or not. There is a passion inside of you for something greater.

WHAT DO YOU FEAR?

The world is before you, and yet here you remain.

Is it failure you fear?
Loneliness?
Change?
The unknown?
Rejection?
Pain?
What holds you back?
What are you holding on to?
What is your excuse?

You can never move forward if you hold onto what you are now. You can never step into the future if you linger in the past.

 Intellectual growth should commence at birth and cease only at death.
~ Albert Einstein

Why is a wounded animal the most dangerous? Why is a hungry lion the one to fear? Because they are weak. Their weakness makes them fierce; it grants them a hunger for survival. Their comfort has been stripped from them, and they must fight to regain it.

Why did the Persians fear the Spartans after the battle of Thermopylae? Because the Spartans surrendered their right to life and victory in order to destroy as many as possible.

They did not fight to win, they simply fought knowing they would lose the battle but in giving the Greeks time to get a massive army together, they knew their sacrifice in the battle would allow the Greeks to defeat the Persians in the war... and they did. The Spartan army surrendered everything that held them back from ferocity, even victory, in order to fight. They fought until their weapons failed them and they were left with their teeth and nails as weapons.

What holds you back?
- Lean into the discomfort!

What satisfies you?
- This is what keeps you coming back for more.

What comforts you?
- This is what keeps you from growing.

What do you fear?
- This is what you should embrace.

A man who wishes to grow strong yet also wishes to be comfortable cannot have both. When he stands in front of the barbell, he must surrender his right to comfort or his longing for strength.

A hero is not great because he is strong; he is great because when he was weak he surrendered his right to himself. Doing so allowed him to hold onto his courage.

You cannot hold onto who you are now and who you wish to become. To do so will destroy you, will make you mediocre.

You must let go of one so you may hold onto the other. Surrender everything that holds you back, and you are free. Free to grow, free to change, free to succeed, and free to fail.

Surrender who you are now and you are free to follow the quiet and steady passion in your heart. This is the art of surrender. Surrender the things that make you weak, and you are only left with what makes you strong.

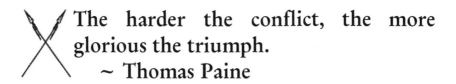 **The harder the conflict, the more glorious the triumph.**
~ Thomas Paine

The hungry, wounded dog is more dangerous than the satisfied lion.

The more you surrender, the less you have to take. The less you have to destroy. The less you have to lose. This makes you strong. This allows you to hold on to what matters.

Become weak. Become hungry. Become thirsty.
When you have nothing left to surrender, then you are ready. Then you are fierce. Then you are brave.

When you have surrendered even your hope of victory and instead hold onto your courage, no amount of failure may stop you.

When you have surrendered your contentment, you are left with only a hunger for growth.

When you have surrendered who you are now, you are free to discover who you may become.

 Great achievement is usually born of great sacrifice, and is never the result of selfishness.
- **Napoleon Hill**

WHAT DO YOU FEAR?

Surely not failure, for failure prepares you for success. Could it be rejection? Surely no, for this makes you examine your motives and actions. Or is it danger of the unknown you fear? Fearing this merely means you are alive and wise, for a fool fears not and a dead man cannot fear at all.

Instead you should fear yourself. Not as you are now, but what you may become. The greatest fire began as a single spark.

WHAT DOES YOUR FUTURE HOLD?

Remain who you are now, and you will never know what you could have been.

Fear change, or fear stagnation.

Hold onto comfort, or hold onto growth.
Surrender your present, or surrender your potential.
Proclaim this among the nations:

"Prepare for war!
Wake up the mighty men,
Let all the men of war draw near,
Let them come up.
Beat your plowshares into swords
And your pruning hooks into spears;
Let the weak say, 'I am strong."
Joel 3:9-10

Fear who you will become, and pray your heart is not misguided.

This is the art of surrender.

*Contribution and acknowledgement to Timothy Baughman

SOLUTION BASED THINKING

What came to be known as Sparta was actually the combining of four villages — Limnae, Pitana, Mesoa and Cynosoura, which are located near what would be the considered Spartan acropolis. These four villages came together to form the early city. This was born from a need to protect a fertile valley of famers that were constantly under attack for their land and their harvest. These four villages came together to protect what they worked so hard for and for an ideology based around hard work, culture, family and community.

WHY SOLUTION BASED THINKING?

Solution Based Thinking or Solution Focused Thinking involves evaluating a current problem or situation and determining a reasonable, practical plan to attack that problem or situation.

THE MINDSET IS...

- There is a solution to this problem or situation

- I possess the skills, talents, and resources to discover the solution

- I will devise a workable plan and make it work.
The following premises are part of solution-focused thinking:

- The focus of thinking and discussion is on the present and the future - not the past.

- The problem is not the focus. What is important is what will be happening when the problem has been eliminated.

- Exceptions are periods when the problem or situation ceases to exist or exists to a lesser degree.

- The problem or situation is not static. Change is inevitable. Positive change is possible.

- Solutions do not always require a major overhaul. Sometimes the smallest of changes is all that is required to create solution to the problem or situation.

- Focusing upon signs of positive change, no matter how small, will result in further positive change to the problem or situation.

- Solution-focused thinking is a collaborative process. Team problem solving may involve: family; co-workers; community members....

HOW DOES SOLUTION-BASED THINKING WORK?

Scaling is an important part of solution-based thinking.

- Ten is how things will be when the problem or situation is resolved. Describe what a ten will look like.

- One is the complete opposite of ten.

Now build a detailed picture of the present situation:

CONSIDER

- What tells you that the problem or situation is not at one?

  At what times does the problem or situation not exist or exists to a lesser extent? When are things better? When is the problem or situation less of a concern?

- What do these times tell you?

- What progress/improvement do you see evidence of, however small?

- What else helps things move toward a ten (external resources; working in a small group; allocation of support...)

NEXT STEPS

Review progress. What is working? Where are setbacks? Identify helpful behaviors. Identify self-defeating behaviors.

DECIDE THE NEXT STEPS

Where Can Solution-Based Thinking be applied?
Solution-based thinking can be applied to any problems or situations you encounter at work, at home, in the community. By focusing on the positive resources and skills a solution-focused approach can enhance the workplace, school, home, or community experience for all members of that environment.

According to de Shazer and Berg (1995) there are three key principles to working in a solutions focused mind set:

1. **If it ain't broke, don't fix it.**

2. **Once you know what works, do more of it.**

3. **If it's not working, do something different.**

WHY IS SOLUTION-FOCUSED THINKING EFFECTIVE?

Instead of dwelling on the problem or situation and obsessing over what isn't, solution-focused thinking sees that because, problems do not occur all of the time, a constructive approach is to discover what is working well and then to do more of it. Rather than dwelling on what isn't or the history of the problem, a solution focused approach looks to the strengths and resources of the individual, team, or organization and how these can be used to generate potential solutions.

This shifts the focus away from problems and towards

useful solutions. Solution-based thinking can and is being applied to such areas as: health, education, community and social care sectors as well as the business and corporate affairs.

PERSONAL DEVELOPMENT

The Spartans were one of the most intellectual and reflective forces on the battlefield of their time. That could be largely attributed to how they saw the battlefield. War was one of the few things the Spartans documented. Throughout their history the Spartan kept very few records but most notably, more than what they didn't keep was what they did keep. The war records were not a testament to pride or victory but rather as a research study throughout the course of events that shaped each battle. The Spartans drew from previous battles to learn the predictive behavior of others, to measure their own efficiency and to forecast their enemy's next move long before it was made. Studying their previous battles also allowed them to find the unpredictable.

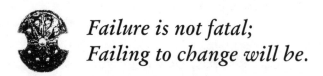

Failure is not fatal;
Failing to change will be.

PERSONAL DEVELOPMENT DELTA

The personal development delta is a common enough idea that is self-triggered, self-managed and self-controlled. The illustration below shows the flow of the delta. The Modern Day Spartan is self-practicing in development. Personal development, group development and discovery does not come from new experiences and much as it comes from new perspective. Self-reflection, reverse engineering and outcome reversal scenarios are paramount to the understanding of personal development.

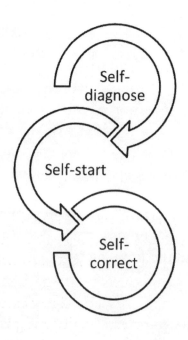

Reverse Engineering

Reverse Engineering is a concept that has been around forever but the process of analyzing the data has become refined and dispensable. In reverse engineering a process, an action, or an outcome, the path is established quite literally by writing down the sequence of events from the ending to the beginning and finding the critical point at which it gave way to less than ideal outcome. The outcome is typically not changed from the expected point but rather many steps backwards in the process.

Example

The application of reverse engineering in a process allows us to draw many examples from practical life. Professional poker players have mastered the art of reverse engineering. As an example, the game of Texas Hold'em has 5 rounds to the pattern. In the pre-betting round players get two cards in which they can quantify their value of the cards and their position in the sequence of the betting. This round is known as the pre-flop. After the first round of betting three cards come out on the table. This round is known as the flop. In this sequence players bet again. Then one card is laid down called the turn. The turn is followed by another round of betting and finally the last card is laid which is called the river. There is one last round of betting and then the players show their cards or fold their hand to superior hand without showing their cards. In poker there is a system called tells. Tells are recorded actions a player remembers that may indicate the strength or weakness of another player and/or their hand. The reason we use this example to demonstrate reverse engineering is because there is a documentable, reversible pattern to draw information from.

When a player is beat by another player and the loser is able to see the hand that beats them, by reverse engineering they can capture and record the sequence of events that lead to the loss.

From the river backwards the loser of the hand will recall the last bet from the winner. How they reacted, how fast or how slow they placed their bet. How they valued their bet. Was it a little bet to entice the player to have to see the final hand? Was it a value bet, which means that after all of the money the player has paid or the value of the bet relative to the amount of money in the pot that there is a statistical probability inclining one to continue.

From the turn backwards, the loser will recall how that hand was bet. How fast, how slow, how much? Did the betting form the turn to the river follow a succession that would make sense relative to the player and the cards on the board?

From the flop the loser will recall all of the same information and consideration and that process will be recorded and recalled all the way to the initial betting of the pre-flop round, the winner's position on the table, the amount of the opening bet, the speed.

In the game of Texas Hold'em it is often times called paying for information when a player is beat in a hand they know they cannot win just to get information that will help them get a better handle or "read" on any particular player in order to have a better understanding of that player.

To further the example, the loss will also prompt that player to recall previous hands and situations whether that player played in the hand or not to get a better understand of their opponents and to have a better understanding of the entire table dynamic.

 "It's a lack of clarity that creates chaos and frustration. Those emotions are poison to any living goal."
~ Unknown

We reference this game as it is one that draws an easy example and one that can be applied to many lessons in life, business and personal development. With the popularity of the game and fanfare attached to it we know we have a larger likelihood of comprehension using this as an illustration. Next time you see the game on television or you are playing the game with friends, think of the process we have illustrated and see if you can record and recall this process of reverse engineering.

After practicing the process you will become more mentally agile and over time you will be able to recall and record with more sophistication. Even in the beginning and potentially forever you may have to write all of the information down. This tactic holds true for professional sports like football and basketball. Players watch film to dissect the moves, plays and predictability of their opponents. The same was true, albeit in a more arcane way back in the time of the Spartans.

In the modern day Reverse Engineering is one of the most practical ways to attack business. Whether it is regarding a client and the way you approach presentations or pitches, if it is regarding employment, both interviewing or being interviewed or if it is applied to the competition in your business. The process of reverse engineering is meant to both study yourself and your predictability and the predictability and sequential action of others.

Six Sigma training encompasses a lot of the fundamentals of business practice improvement and new practice development through the science of reverse engineering. The idea is to document a process and work it in reverse order.

One of the most impactful parts of reverse engineering comes from the new process development. Here the process is a little different in the sense that all of the parts that come before a particular outcome may not be known. However, starting with an end in mind and working backwards to assess what must happen directly before accomplishing an outcome will help you work all the way to the starting point in order to capture a new process. If we are always building a process for improvement with the end in mind and refining the steps that is takes to get there we will find ourselves more inclined to succeed. Much like the Spartan's mentality of battle, this process will show us a path, potential pitfalls, and opportunities for improvement.

"If you always do what you've always done you will always get you have always gotten."
~ Unknown

PROCESS CAPTURE

The second end of reverse engineering is probably the most impactful and that is process capture. Doing it is great, capturing it so you can train, delegate or provide a concise way for others to do it is even more meaningful.

In our Spartan training we focus heavily on this idea. The Spartan Intrapreneur understands $500 per hour work. We use this expression in our training all the time and here is what it means. When a Modern Day Spartan is identified we surround them with the principles of balance, focus, organization and goals. We want all Modern Day Spartans to think like millionaires. We make sure to focus on the fact that the drive for money without balance is flawed so we promote the 40 hour work week in this equation. That being said, $500 per hour work is based on the premise that in order to earn $1,000,000 per year on a 40 hour work week, one would need to make $500 per hour. That is where we focus when we think about how to achieve our goals of balance and in the work place we tend to do more to create the illusion of being busy instead of creating the reality of outcome. The balanced millionaire mind will measure their output and attach a financial value to the work that they do. In order to be a millionaire you must think like a millionaire and what I am sure of is no millionaire in the world is out there doing $10 per hour work. What this means is if you find yourself doing work that doesn't measure up to the value you have attached to yourself then you had better figure out one of two things; either how to Automate or Innovate.

 Innovation is taking two things that already exist and putting them together in a new way.
~ Tom Freston

We encourage the impact of a time study. This is a critical component of reverse engineering. You have to be able to see things in reverse and the best way to do that is to physically capture your own process. This exercise usually gets a pretty good laugh and a little shame as well when it is done thoroughly. Here is how it is done. Begin by writing out what your $500 per hour tasks look like. What are all of things you could be doing that would be equal to the value you have put on your best work. After writing that list then you capture everything down to the granular detail that you did in a day and you repeat this process for an entire week. At the end of the week pull out that original list of your highest value work and compare that to what you actually did. You will notice that while you may have executed some million dollar tasks you worked a lot of hours for little or no money due to either being unfocused, unplanned or simply because you were doing work better suited for someone else. Once you can simplify your work and only focus on the high impact portions of what you do you will notice a lot of free time has been afford to you that can be spent on these tasks. We are often met with objections in this study by people saying that they do not have someone else to do the remedial or mundane tasks but we assure you if this is what you are focusing on you are not seeing the forest for the trees.

In my early sales career I remember sitting at an awards ceremony where I won the rookie of the year distinction in sales. Shortly after I was awarded my acknowledgement, the company had moved on to their sales person of the year, the grandest distinction of them all. What had dawned on my when they were reviewing the numbers was that she had out performed me by 500%. I thought to myself... "That is impossible". How could I possibly be 500% more effective than I was already being? I was working 60 – 80 hours per week and no matter how I could scale it in my mind the accomplishment seemed impossible. That was until I heard this woman give her acceptance speech.

I remember when she received her award she thanked every department in the company, and many individually within these departments, and with reason. She had thanked each department and specific people in their respective departments for doing her work for her. When I heard this I was intrigued. She went into great detail about what she had had all of these different people doing for her. She had people in all of these departments doing the same work I was doing myself. I thought surely this must have been some kind of privilege she was granted because she was so good.

Without leaps of imagination, or dreaming, we lose the excitement of possibilities. Dreaming, after all, is a form of planning.
~ Gloria Steinam

After the event I remember talking to her and asking her how had this had come to be. She explained to me that there were people in this company that could do portions of her job for her and do it better, faster and more efficiently than she could ever do herself. She had told me she was not hired to manage these things but to manage those that were. She had also explained that when she shared her victories with these teams it promoted their value within the organization and no one would be crazy enough to tell her she couldn't be using people in this fashion. Instead, I was astonished at how she was praised by the entire organization for doing just that.

These resources are all around you. A Modern Day Spartan must first walk the path in order to understand the benefit and the pain. They must also understand we are gifted with the knowledge that many of the rules we assume are merely interpretations by ourselves (and sometimes by others) to give us confidence and assurance in our own ideology. An ideology that leads to a convenience of limitation. Challenge everything but before you reach your conclusion you must always be sure to ask yourself this...

Have you walked the gauntlet?
~ Kent McClelland

PART 2

THE MODERN
DAY SPARTAN
"IN BUSINESS"

INTRODUCING THE SPARTAN "INTRAPRENEUR"

While the term Intrapreneur is not new, the application certainly is. The Spartan's were certainly the first Intrapreneur. The Intrapreneur is not someone who runs from organization to create a better version of where they were but someone who stays within the organization to better where they are. The Spartans understood democracy and embrace sharing thoughts and ideas as a culture. These thoughts and ideas were not competing to finds the best idea but instead combining to find the best ideas. Often in Spartan law and battle, collectives were gathered both on the battle field and in their Agora (village square) so that the people could brainstorm and strategize their challenges and concerns together. We believe this was the true essence of Sparta's success as we believe this is also the true essence of the Intrapreneur. The idea that one idea is good but that many ideas combined are better, more refined and more impactful.

WHY THE SPARTAN INTRAPRENEUR?

The Intrapreneur has to channel their Modern Day Spartan and be both strategic in their thinking, inventive in their attack and inclusive in their thoughts. Not all of their ideas will be embraced nor will their thinking. Not because they are wrong but because they are breaking from tradition. The Modern Day Spartan is on a mission to create an inclusion, a healthy and active lifestyle full of balance and they strive to bring out the best in people. They are fearless and persistent in everything and every person they touch.

These days it's typically the entrepreneur that gets the glory; the smart start-up guy who seems to know what the next big thing will be, the social savvy app developer that is suddenly all over our iOs, the Kickstarted inventor, whose idea just might change the world. But in reality, these guys have one-in-a-million chance of really creating a stir, establishing themselves as professionals in their industry, or making a real impact on society (not to mention their family's social mobility). In the real world, the place most of us, our wives and kids, live, it's the Intrapreneur who makes the biggest difference; who rises to the top and makes his mark on his industry, furthers his career, and improves his world by providing for his family.

What is an Intrapreneur?

An Intrapreneur is a person who takes an entrepreneurial attitude and applies that kind of enthusiasm, interest, creativity and innovation to their 9 to 5 jobs. Much like the Spartans individuality was critical to the team but collaboration was the true sense of the Spartan. Collaboration in effort to make the team stronger held more honor than the idea of a lone wolf or being the strongest individual. The strength and success of Sparta came from the entire team.

Forbes magazine refers to the Intrapreneur as "the heroes" at work, because they're the game changers within their organizations. The Intrapreneur is the bosses' best friend, the person they come to trust the most, and thus promote above anyone else. The Intrapreneur doesn't own the business; he just feels ownership over his career.

It's that sense of ownership over one's work and life that leads the Intrapreneur to success. These are the kind of people that become indispensable to their workplaces. Their companies literally cannot afford to lose them, thus the Intrapreneur doesn't have to chase after raises and promotions, rather, the money and just success naturally follows.

The Spartan Intrapreneur

The Spartan Intrapreneur is a hybrid modern-day warrior and innovator. His primary competition at his work is himself, and he is constantly striving to up his game. He's fearless when it comes to tackling new assignments and taking his office in bold, new directions. That fear of failure isn't cocky bravado though; rather it comes from an innate understanding of his capabilities. And the Spartan Intrapreneur knows that even failure comes with its own set of invaluable lessons.

Constantly anticipating several steps ahead of his colleagues, the Spartan Intrapreneur revels in challenge, rather than dreads the toil that every position occasionally entails. The Spartan Intrapreneur is able to reframe mundane tasks, as even the most tedious drudgery can be training for a keener sense of self-discipline.

Above all else, when engaged in work, the Spartan Intrapreneur is focused and persistent. You don't see him wasting his employer's time playing games or procrastinating. His career and his duty to the commitment he made when he accepted his position is far too important to him. His potential to achieve is only limited by the resources made available to him, and the Spartan Intrapreneur is adept at making the most out of the hand he's been dealt.

Finally, balance is key to the modern-day Spartan Intrapreneur, and he sees maintaining that balance between work and family, rest and engagement, as essential to his battle plan. When any aspect of his personal life begins to interfere with his efforts to perform his duties to the best of his ability, he immediately responds to remedy the situation. He is not afraid to put in the work or alter course if necessary when it comes to personal or working relationships. His guiding principles in all of his interactions tend to be integrity and authenticity, and he strives to always speak and act with his values in mind.

The essence of the Spartan Intrapreneur makes him a crucial player for any business to distinguish itself in the competitive market. The willingness to go to battle, not just for his company's brand, but for the sake of his career and sense of pride that comes with his accomplishments, is the vital difference that sets apart mercenary middle management from the genuine gladiators of the corporate world.

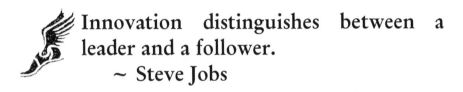 **Innovation distinguishes between a leader and a follower.**
~ Steve Jobs

What goes on in the mind of an Intrapreneur? In a recent study, researchers compared the elements related to entrepreneurial and intrapreneurial activity. The study found that among the 32,000 subjects who participated in it, five percent were engaged in the initial stages of a business startup, either on their own or within an organization. The study also found that human capital such as education and experience is connected more with entrepreneurship than with intrapreneurship. Another observation was that intrapreneurial startups were inclined to concentrate more on business-to-business products while entrepreneurial startups were inclined towards consumer sales and/or services.

Another important difference between entrepreneurship

and intrapreneurship is age. The study found that people who launched their own companies were in their thirties and forties. People from older and younger age groups were risk averse or felt they had no opportunities for entrepreneurships. This makes them perfect candidates for intrapreneurship experiences.

Entrepreneurship appeals to people who possess natural traits that find startups exciting. Intrapreneurs generally would not like to get entangled in startups. They don't want the bother and the risk. Managers will help their companies if they are on the lookout for employees who have the interest and potential to develop new ideas. All they need is the time, the resources and the encouragement to turn ideas into reality.

 The price of greatness is responsibility.
~ Winston Churchill

All the talent in the world won't take you to the top of your game or a business. In order to be successful, you have to have the will to work hard, work smart and have the belief that you will succeed.

You need the right mindset and a continuous "can do" attitude. Start your day out with positive reading and quiet time first thing in the morning. I like to clear my mind and visualize the things I want to accomplish for the day. It is important that you stay positive and make a difference daily at work and home.

You have to have the mindset of a great leader. Create an environment that allows people to flourish. Have humility and understanding for others, regardless of your title or education, your wealth or your status. Have an attitude of Gratitude and strive to be your best daily.

To make a change in the outer expression of your business, you need to create new habits within the inner working of your mind. To do this, I use a tool called affirmative statements or positive affirmations.

Self-affirmations are positive statements or self-scripts that can condition the subconscious mind to help you develop a more positive perception of yourself. Affirmations can help you to change harmful behaviors or accomplish goals, and they can also help undo the damage caused by negative scripts, those things which we repeatedly tell ourselves (or which others repeatedly tell us) that contribute to a negative self-perception. Affirmations are easy to create and use, but you'll need dedication to make them work.

Affirmative statements can have two basic uses, depending on which meaning is being applied. When its grammatical meaning is being applied, an affirmative statement can be used to state any basic fact. In conversation, it allows the speaker to verbally express agreement.

In self-development, an affirmative statement builds confidence. It helps the speaker get into a successful mind set. Affirmative statements also help you put things in priority—organize your day.

It is a good practice to write affirmations and put them

somewhere you will see them. They will be an encouragement whenever you read them. They help you keep that positive mind set and your goals in front of you all day.

 If you think you can do a thing or think you can't do a thing, you're right. ~ Henry Ford

I would suggest you use the self-affirming statements below:

- I trust in myself and all that I attract to guide me.

- I make decisions effortlessly. The "how" always appears.

- I transform any invisible blocks and limiting thoughts into limitless fuel.

- The vision of my business is solid and whole.

- My growing team and I are powerfully aligned and attract everything we need, when we need it.

- The daily practice of repeating positive thought changing statements have a definite positive impact on your "intended outcomes".

THE INTRAPRENEUR MODEL

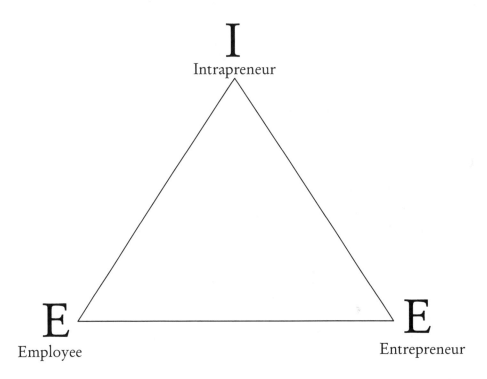

Many employees think the leap to success comes from putting in their time and relying on seniority to pave their path to growth. Some succeed on this path and work their way to the top. Others (many others) face the alternative. They also rely on the same sequence of events to happen to them but are later let down when someone else surpasses them or leap frogs them in their effort to work hard and put in their time. It gets even worse when the company hires from outside to fill the position above them. This often creates resentment or frustration within this person towards the company. Like many things that do not go our way, people will often tend to point the blame at the organization or thing that overlooked them. The reality in both business and in life is the same. If you feel like you were missed for an opportunity when you were next in line than you need to look at yourself. Identify what you did wrong or what you didn't do at all. What did you miss? Were you the best version of yourself or did you think that you would succeed from showing up to work every day and doing your job? Even worse, did you think you were entitled to what you wanted or what you felt you deserved? This is an employee.

Often times when an employee is misunderstood or looked over it is common for that employee to make a leap. One with the logic that says if these people can't see my potential then I will go somewhere else where they do. The cycle will repeat itself until eventually the employee comes to the conclusion that they are either the cause of their own fate and they strive to correct their misdirection or they will go out on their own to prove everyone wrong and create their own fate. This can then leads to that employee becoming an entrepreneur.

There are of course natural born entrepreneurs that never worked for any type of organization their entire life. These people are the exception. It can be wiring it can be handed down from generation to generation but this is the exception not the rule.

Enter the Intrapreneur. This is the employee with the entrepreneur mindset, drive and objective to improve, enhance and evolve their current shared environment. The risk is low and the reward is high in their mind. It isn't their money or resources at risk. Eventhough this is not the thought process for their decision making process it is true nonetheless.

We write the equation and the success path from the model illustrated above like this.

- **Employee** – <u>Low Risk/Low yield.</u>
  "Play it safe and things will eventually happen."

- **Entrepreneur** – <u>High Risk/High Yield.</u>
  "Drive fast, take chances... it will eventually pay off."

- **Intrapreneur** – <u>Low Risk/High Yield.</u>
  "I know my worth and I have the results to prove what I propose. If my company doesn't understand that, I made a mistake in selecting them as the place in which I thought I could improve."

Intrapreneurs have a very distinct mindset that sets them apart from an employee. They never play "not to lose", but instead... "they play to win!". It may seem like semantics but there is a very large difference.

One mentality defends and plays it safe never taking calculated risks. "Just maintain and manage."

The other is on offence, leading with new ideas, cutting edge innovation and depth in teamwork and sharing in both victory and defeat. The Intrapreneur is accountable! "We don't manage, we lead!"

FEATURES OF INTRAPRENEURSHIP

Intrapreneurship involves innovation, the ability to take risk and creativity. An entrepreneur will be able to look at things in novel ways. He will have the capacity to take calculated risks and to accept failure as a learning experience. An Intrapreneur thinks like an entrepreneur looking out for opportunities which profit his organization. Intrapreneurship is a novel way of making organizations more profitable where imaginative employees entertain entrepreneurial thoughts. It is in the interest of an organization to encourage Intrapreneurs.

Intrapreneurship is a significant method for companies to reinvent themselves and improve performance.
The idea can be scary and may seem to look a little like anarchy but the best people in business know that it is the people in their business that make their business. If there were no need for the human element and creative thinking all business would be automated.

Intrapreneurship can take several forms within the walls of any business. Intrapreneurs are typically more autonomous than the typical employee. They seek to challenge the conventional wisdom. They tend to question the legacy rules that exist in most companies. When they are told to do something a certain way, they may often enquire to know why. When they are told "because it is the way we have always done things", they tend to question that as well.

Everything starts with your thoughts and your beliefs. It

starts NOW! Know that there is no separation in your life or in your business. Eat, sleep, and live your vision.

Lastly, understand that the Modern Day Spartan is not a revolution, it is an evolution. You can revolt for change but change is evolution and it is the change that matters. Fight less to change those around you and focus more on changing yourself. You will see that when you change yourself, positive things will happen and you will attract positive people. At the end of the day the best people always win out!

BRAVE NEW WORK PLACE

The eventual downfall of the great Spartan civilization came from an inability to adapt to a changing environment.   In converse to how the Spartans used their physical environment to adapt strength, tactics and strategies this was merely a practice used in a static environment but as the world around the Spartans changed with a heavier influence on politics and religion, the Spartans did not know how to evolve. They could not change their dynamic thinking or apply static logic to a dynamic principle. They had all of the tools and the mindset but in the end it was their arrogance that was their downfall. All of the once great principles they had used to develop their civilization had grown foggy and calloused due to their arrogance. They stopped letting people into Sparta. They were constantly in a state of paranoia and leery of any outsider that would enter their domain. And soon they became extinct without capturing their history in writing or very little of it any way. They great Sparta finally gave way and dissolved due to their inability to evolve and their own foolish pride.

The modern day Spartan doesn't just draw their motivation from the success principles of the past but also from its failures.

There are many old world Spartans around us today...everywhere we look. You can find them in business, in your family, amongst your friends and even in our popular culture. They can be our ministers, our doctors, our judges. These are the people that stand in the way of evolution, progress and a changing landscape.

These are the people that are emboldened from the past. Those that live a life predicated on what we call Legacy Rules. Legacy Rules are those that state we will always do things the way we have always done things because they have worked. As younger generations come up, these legacy rules are falling to the wayside faster than you can say Legacy Rules.

To be crazy enough to think that all of the innovation, change and evolution that has happened in the business world in the last decade, year or even month will yield to yesterday's rules will only get one devoured by this change. It will not stop it, slow it down or even cause the change to notice. This evolution will continue to give way to the modern day Spartan. It will continue to give way to the Intrapreneur.

The intrapreneurial mindset helps drive innovation and uncover opportunities within the challenges of operating in a changing world.
A key asset of the Intrapreneur is their ability to think

"inside" of the box. You heard correct! Thinking outside of the box usually means reinventing the wheel. The Intrapreneur would prefer to take a system, process or operation that currently exists and through insight, collaboration and creativity, instead choose to make it better, faster, smarter and easier to engage with.

CEOs will attest to the fact that the success of their company often hinges on hiring and providing a nurturing environment for its Intrapreneurs.

The concept of being an Intrapreneur is not new. It was first coined in a paper by Gifford and Elizabeth Pinchot back in 1978. In 1992, The American Heritage Dictionary included it as a part of North American vocabulary.

 Thinking is the hardest work there is, which is probably the reason why so few engage in it.
~ Henry Ford

An Intrapreneur works inside a large corporation. In that environment, the Intrapreneur accepts responsibility for taking an idea—which may or may not have originated with the Intrapreneur—and turning it from a paper concept into a concrete, finished product. To do this, the Intrapreneur uses creative problem solving, innovation, and risk-taking.

An Intrapreneur—and the company for whom he/she works—has to make an attitudinal shift from what we consider the "traditional employee" or "legacy employee" to becoming self-promoting, self-initiating, and willing to take risks.

This is a major change in the employee-employer relationship. It is a major change in the business world altogether.

Traditional Employee-Employer Relationship

Historically, employer-employee relations in western culture involved a "psychological contract" between employer and employees. The workers made a long-term commitment to the company or organization or employer. In exchange, the worker received long-term job security, training and development. Inherent in that "contract" was the possibility (stated or inferred) for opportunities for promotion within the company.

All that changed in the early seventies when recession hit businesses. Organizations began using extensive downsizing to cut costs. Outsourcing became a way to decrease the number of permanent employees in the workforce and thus to cut the costs of full-time employee wages, benefits, and retirement plans.

With this shift came a change in employees-employer relations. Instead of being eager and industrious about promotion in the corporation, many employees began to plan how to shift to another more secure corporation.

Many also began to consider small business startups. Several things were responsible for this employer-employee relations shift. Large numbers of permanent employees make dealing with business downturns next to impossible. Unionized workers cannot be made to take pay decreases. Legislation also protects them from dismissal. All this has increased corporate desire to use outsourcing and hire short-term, temporary, contract-only, and leased employees to make downsizing immediately possible and lawsuit-free.

The push for higher returns on investment, declines in hiring, increases in layoffs, the boom of IPOs and shortage of funds for employee on-the-job training have all strained the traditional employer-employee relationship.

Rather than feeling a company "family" loyalty, employees have begun to see it as a "them-against-us" relationship where the employer tries to squeeze more work for less remuneration from a shrinking staff. Employees have become critical of employers. Employee morale and commitment and motivation have all taken a nose dive.

Due the change in the employee/employer relationship, economic conditions, and basically "Legacy Thinking", the average person today is said will have 7 careers in their lifetime. That is a far change from the 1 to 2 careers a person would have just 30 years ago. A common mindset amongst employees today is to get in at a ground level opportunity relative to the career they want and exchange your way up through multiple companies until you reach the desired status and security you have been looking for. This has become transparent to employers and in response they have had to change the way they value an employee.

The reality is: Many jobs have gone to third-world

countries where wages are low and benefits are non-existent. At the same time, North American employees are now working fifteen percent more hours per week than they were two decades ago. Sales people are being asked to increase sales while their employers have cut travel, phone, and advertising budgets. Moreover employers couch the changes in high sounding language that is intended to delude employees with euphemistic jargon used to justify the changes being implemented. Clearly, in many businesses, employee-employer relations lack trust and confidence.

 You must be the change you wish to see in the world.
~ Mahatma Gandhi

This changing landscape is giving way to a new mindset...

THE INTRAPRENEUR-EMPLOYER RELATIONSHIP

Ideally, the employer sees opportunities for improving his company in nurturing the qualities and output of the Intrapreneur. The employer recognizes the value of Intrapreneurs to employee morale and to the bottom line of his company. The savvy employer also knows that more than cash, what spurs on an Intrapreneur is encouragement, recognition and autonomy.

Employers who recognize their Intrapreneurs and make wise use of them are those who first have a clear vision they can articulate about what the company stands for, where it is going and what will help it get there. With this framework in place, the Intrapreneur can thrive.

Intrapreneurs are inspired by visionary leaders who can describe the company vision. Then it is simply a matter of providing the creative space and a welcoming environment.

Good business leaders create a vision, articulate the vision, passionately own the vision, and relentlessly drive it to completion.
~ Jack Welch quotes

Employees who show initiative and are given ten or fifteen percent of their work day to work on new ideas, processes, products, and/or and services immediately get the message that they are needed, valued, and appreciated. The plain and simple truth is: employees tend to work harder on the things they like doing.

Today's employers brainstorm with employees, and challenge them to develop innovations on their own time. These thoughts/suggestions are then shared at company informal meetings. Intrapreneurs are encouraged to add suggestions for improvements on processes, routines, feedback, client relations...
Even if the Intrapreneurs idea flops down the road, it is still

crucial that you reward his or her effort. You may choose, for example, to give that employee a certificate of appreciation and a dinner at a nice restaurant. The bottom line is that whether you decide on percentage points, promotions or other fancy perks, it helps to give your employees a reason to take a chance on their ideas.

THE MIND SET OF AN INTRAPRENEUR: CHARACTERISTICS

Every company has employees that go beyond the call of duty. There are employees who are energized by opportunities to improve processes, products or services. Intrapreneurs are inspired because they believe they can make a difference to the company, the community, perhaps even the world! While a comprehensive list will never include every quality of an Intrapreneur.

Here are some glimpses into the mind of the Intrapreneur:

• Intrapreneurs have lots of ideas and are enthusiastic about them.

• Intrapreneurs possess a vast knowledge of their environment. They may be engineers, technicians, scientists, mathematicians. They see relationships among things.

• Intrapreneurs have a vision and a desire to change things for the better.

• Intrapreneurs are team players who can lead and inspire others.

• Intrapreneurs have a network of support people on whom they can call.

• Intrapreneurs don't give up. Setbacks are merely challenges to persevere

• Intrapreneurs cherish change.

• Intrapreneurs are persistent in the face of complications. They love a good challenge.

• Intrapreneurs have passion and high motivation to make things happen.

• Intrapreneurs are persuasive and encouraging of their teammates.

• Intrapreneurs have a strong customer focus. They look for ways to get a job done that considers customers. His mindset is client-focused.

• Intrapreneurs see opportunities. They envision the possibilities where others see only obstacles.

• Intrapreneurs are flexible. If needed, they can change their aims and objectives for the good of the project, organization, or client.

• Intrapreneurs see their job not as a duty but rather as an opportunity to effect change.

• Intrapreneurs do not face risks of entrepreneurs. They have corporate support. However, they are willing to risk security and potentially having others resist their ideas. They may even risk their jobs.

• Intrapreneurs have high self-confidence. They are so sure they are right and are pursuing a righteous cause that they will risk insubordination. The chain of command is not a popular concept for Intrapreneurs.

• Intrapreneurs will not duck responsibility by saying it is "not in my job description". Intrapreneurs will do whatever it takes. In that way, they think like owners of the business.

• Intrapreneurs are loyal to their employers and the company. Intrapreneurs have frequently worked their entire career for the same company—or the one that bought it out.

How Do You Nurture an Intrapreneurial Mindset in Your Organization?

We've all seen and chuckled at the cartoon where the Intrapreneur presents his idea to his immediate superior who commends him and then announces that he has to "run it up the corporate ladder". At each of the six steps on that ladder is an individual who, fearing the effect of that innovative idea trims, hacks, cuts, alters, and tweaks the idea. It is returned to the Intrapreneur bearing little resemblance to the innovative idea he had proffered.

Obviously this is not the way to nurture an Intrapreneur. Large corporations like IBM, AT&T, General Electric, General Motors, General Mills, and of course Google, have discovered the value of providing incentives to their intrapreneurial employees. It is a valuable lesson for business owners at companies of all sizes. Every enterprise, organization, or non-profit can benefit from nurturing its Intrapreneurs. How do they go about encouraging, shaping, and molding their creativity?

How can companies establish the lines of responsibility for intrapreneurial employees and their projects? How can forward-thinking leaders develop an intrapreneurial spirit within their organization?

The intrapreneurial mindset flourishes when positive energy in the workplace creates a positive environment. In a book by Matthew Dixon and Brent Adamson, it discusses the idea of the "Commander's Intent". The principle comes from the military. It knows that no matter how much training a soldier endures, when it comes to it, battle instinct will always override training. It is with that that the commander will give the needed outcome and by hook or crook, training or instinct, the men will arrive at the needed endpoint. The commander's intent in Sparta was that of honor, fear of shame and teamwork. If all else was lost on the battle field, the men would all come together because they all knew the commander's intent. This idea of the commander's intent is the essence of managing the Intrapreneur.

This leads, eventually, to positive results.

Ingrid Vanderveldt, an entrepreneur-in-residence at Dell: "Intrapreneurship can be just as impactful and certainly just as critical as entrepreneurship. That same drive, creativity and passion for growth that entrepreneurs have can be used inside a company to benefit customers and team members."

Creativity requires the courage to let go of certainties.
~ Erich Fromm

There are growing pains involved. By their very nature, corporations are conservative and cautious. They prefer the road well-traveled. Unfortunately, the well-worn paths leave little room for an Intrapreneur to flex, speculate, explore, dabble, and create and try new ideas and innovations. In most organizations the relation between the Intrapreneur and the company decision makers is at best uneasy.

Many Intrapreneurs get tired of the red tape, the bureaucratic turf protecting and go out on their own. Many entrepreneurs started as an under-appreciated Intrapreneur.

Intrapreneurs need to feel heard, recognized, encouraged, and supported.

A work environment that fosters intrapreneurial employees has a clear reward system. For most Intrapreneurs, it's not about money, though money is an important recognition for their accomplishments. A percent of the profits resulting from his or her product, a bonus, a tangible reward like in lieu days, or other recognition need not be a costly idea.

Here is an example: The inventor of Post-It Notes got no money for his idea. What he did get was a promotion, a pay raise and company benefits.

Make sure the reward will be viewed as a reward. Giving someone who loves field work a desk promotion would not be perceived as a reward by an Intrapreneur. Since it is not a good fit, it might not be a plus for the enterprise either.

A WONDERFUL LESSON IN INTRAPRENUERSHIP.

In her early career Karyn Dill was the marketing director for the American Heart Association. With a lack of a local direct report Karyn had autonomy and she understood her job and its demand as merely "Commander's Intent". She knew her job was based on the performance, brand awareness and revenue generation. A perfect example of the Intrapreneur came from a story she told me of an event that she was going to for the Downtown Billings Association Christmas parade. This was in Billings, MT and she was calling the event "A Cowboy Christmas".

The idea was to have Santa wearing a cowboy hat and cowboy boots along with the traditional red and white suit while driving an old stage coach with horses full of presents instead of the traditional sleigh and reindeer. She was told she didn't have the budget nor would she be able to find a stage coach for rent that would hold up to the demand of the parade route. They were just for show, she was told. She thought clearly in a state like Montana there must be a stage coach in working order on every other ranch. After looking for months to no avail the time came when, on the way back from an event in rural Montana, she and her colleagues drove by an old farmhouse with a stage coach in the front yard on display. Karyn had instructed the driver to turn around because she was going to get that stagecoach for the parade. Her colleagues had commented that it wouldn't work. They gave her a litany of reasons why: It was broken down and that these people wouldn't rent or loan her such a prized possession. They would likely shoot her if she stepped foot on their property and rang the doorbell. It was a few hundred miles away from Billing and she couldn't possibly get it back there in one piece.

Never one to listen to people telling her she couldn't do something, she went to the door of the old farm house, told them what she was up to and the people had said, we would let you borrow it, but the frame is unstable and there is no way to move it. She had countered with an offer, stating that if she were to arrange freight and have the chasse re-welded and woodwork fixed to be in working order for exchange of her using it (for free) in the parade, would they then be willing to let her use it? The owners conceded with great joy knowing that the biggest city in the state would be featuring their stage coach in a televised parade and that in return for doing pretty much nothing they would get it back in full working order, a condition they admitted it had never been in since they owned it.

The deal was done. Karyn had a friend from college that owned a trucking company. He picked up and loaded the stage coach for free and shipped it down to another friend that had a woodworking and welding shop. The metal supports were rebuilt and welded, the wooden frame made in exacting fashion to the original and reinforced it with steel struts. The event went off without a hitch. The fundraiser was very impressive and it was all done by a forward thinking Intrapreneur who only needed Commander's Intent.

 The secret to creativity is knowing how to hide your sources.
~ Albert Einstein

EXEMPLARY PRACTICES

Some successful companies have been particularly innovative in devising ways to recognize their entrepreneurs and/or for implementing a culture that nurtures its Intrapreneurs.

Programs that identify, coach, and facilitate Intrapreneurs include: Toyota, Macdonald's, Dreamworks, Facebook, and LinkedIn. Innovative leaders encourage Intrapreneurs to turn their ideas into new processes, products and/or services that save the company time, money, resources and/or improve customer services or the customer experience.

Skunkworks has turned Intrapreneurial initiatives into a whole new environment. Their workers are given a lot of autonomy to work on advanced research and development. If the development project is successful, it will eventually go through the production stage.

Companies like 3M, Google ad Atlassian also provide an environment where employees are given freedom to decide how, where, and with whom they work.
As far back as 1930, 3M gave employees 15% of their time to work on innovations that would save the company time and/or money. Google's one day per week for working on innovations has produced an intrapreneurial half of its creative projects including: Google Maps, Gmail and Google News.

Atlassian, the Australian Software Company challenges its employees to "deliver" new products, services, or processes "overnight" on Fed-Ex Day held four times a year.

THE IMPORTANCE OF INTRAPRENEURS

Intrapreneurs help companies remain current and solvent. Intrapreneurs infuse energy into new business ventures. If companies do not actively promote intrapreneurship, they die. If you are looking for proof of this, you need look no farther than Kodak and RIM. Both rested on the laurels of previously wildly popular products while companies like Cannon and Apple continued to pour money into intrapreneurial ventures to change with the times. Perhaps if Kodak and Rim had put emphasis on evolving, their products and companies would not be in jeopardy today.

These companies are moving the way of Sparta. With their legacy rules, arrogance and inability to evolve, they will be left to ruin much like Sparta too.

It is extremely important for education to offer basics of entrepreneurship and intrapreneurship skills. Not every student will become the next Steve Jobs or Bill Gates. That's not important. Teaching skills necessary for success as an Intrapreneur can help companies by preparing a work force that can apply intrapreneurial skills to the specific needs of the company. Those who have these valuable skills are capable of putting their enterprise on the map with innovative processes, services, and products. This changing work environment and these people are the essence of the Modern Day Spartan.

BRANDING

&

PROMOTION

Basically, a brand is an idea and perceived value formed by its intended audience based on a company's culture, product, and service.

Regardless of whether we ever intended to become involved in marketing, we are all involved in marketing or branding ourselves. Each and every day you put your personal brand on what you do, what you aim to do, how you do it, and how you treat others.

Marketing or branding involves how you present yourself to those around you: at work, in your home, and in your community. Your personal brand is the you that you consistently offer those who come into contact with you. Branding affects the work you do, the parent, spouse, child you present to your family, and the friendships you provide for others to experience, enjoy, use, or "consume" to use a marketing term.

When you are marketing or branding yourself, you are consciously building that experience so that you can effectively get what you want in return from your life: success, money, love, confidence, and self-fulfillment.

That's what marketing truly is all about. When you brand yourself you create a consistent experience for your clients. Keep in mind these clients are colleagues, bosses, family, friends, and yes, paying clients!

Ask yourself: Are you a "big brand" or are you just managing your life toward your own personal goals?

We live by a motto that we do not work for anyone. We work with people. A company may employee us but that does not mean we work for them. The idea of working with them is an understanding that both parties bring value to the table. You provide a service to a company and that company pays you in kind. Getting in line with this kind of self-worth and value statement is an imperative in the pivot point to successful self-branding and marketing.

The key here is to take control. You are your own brand manager. You have to set the course for your own brand experience. It's your show. In order to be successful you have to love your brand.

When scoping out their business models and marketing plans, all the big brands analyze and decide what they are good at and what they want to develop. Big brands pull together an inventory of skills that could possibly make them who they are. Then they brand themselves.

As your own personal brand manager, you need to take inventory. What are you good at? What skills can you sell to clients? Until you define you brand you cannot possibly market yourself effectively.

Ask yourself: How is my brand unique. How can my brand "out sell" all others? How can I build a product or service unlike all the others in my field?

So the first step is to define who you want to be as a person. We can't move ahead without knowing what we want out of life. Every brand does it. So can you.

 For a truly effective social campaign, a brand needs to embrace the first principles of marketing, which involves brand definition and consistent storytelling.
~ Simon Mainwaring

Things to think about:

• What are your personal skills, talents, and your attributes and the ones you want to acquire over time?

• Are these skills, talents, and attributes realistic? Are they attainable?

• Can you use these skills, talents, attributes to differentiate yourself from your competition?

- Most importantly: Will these skills bring you success, happiness, and satisfaction?

Start by outlining all the areas of your life where you want to achieve success and happiness. This would certainly include your career, but also your social life, relationships, family life, and places you would want to live. It's never too early to start a bucket list. Your goal should be directly linked to your brand and ultimately, your master plan.
Remember: Your personal brand should be a projection, a long-range plan for what you want out of life, and not necessarily where you are right now.

Creating your personal brand is just a start. We need to turn this into a positioning for your brand so that it serves as a guide for how you build your brand.

This is the first step on the way to loving your brand.
A company or person without a brand may have a feeling about how things should be but have not captured a process of how things should be seen and felt by others. Without self-branding, we are working in the dark.

WHAT DOES IT MEAN TO PROMOTE YOURSELF?

Promoting oneself involves adopting behaviors and activities that ensure that people know who you are. They are aware of your skills, your talents, and your goals.

Businesses that know the importance of Intrapreneurs to the wellbeing of their enterprise are always on the lookout for employees who possess the spirit of an entrepreneur.

This is a competitive world. It is not enough to be incredibly creative and full of great ideas. You have to let the world know you have these skills, abilities, and talents and you are eager to use them.

If you know what job you want, you need to pursue it proactively. Other less talented people who know how to promote themselves will get the job you want because they went out and actively sought it.

If you want to be recognized within an organization for your intrapreneurial potential, you need to let your light shine within that company. If you know what you want, get out there and pursue your goals proactively.

 A brand for a company is like a reputation for a person. You earn reputation by trying to do hard things well.
~ Jeff Bezos

Networking is one of the best ways to promote yourself, your talents and your professional goals. This includes getting known within your company by participating in company initiatives and getting the attention of the movers in your organization. It also means associating with others in like businesses through your industry's professional associations, meetings, seminars, workshops, and/or conferences.

Socializing is another good way to promote yourself. If your workplace offers social groups, house sports leagues, committees, interoffice activities, make a point of getting actively involved or be proactive in starting them.

Socializing also has a secondary meaning or iteration. To socialize oneself is understood but when you are a brand you are socializing other people to your brand, making them aware that you are greater than the sum of your parts. It also means getting them familiar with the consistency of you as both a person and a brand.

If the terms, "networking" and "socializing" scare you, get over it. Your inhibitions will hold you back. If you are shy or introverted, work on leaning into the discomfort! We cannot get better without overcoming fear. We don't suggest that you live in the discomfort but you certainly must lean in. Find a way to socialize your discomfort. When things are not productive for us we often use the idea of innovate or automate. Some things may simply not be for us. It is with the understanding and the familiarity of these things that we can capitalize on our resources to do some of that work for us. Regardless, you have to put yourself out there!

Place yourself in situations like community get-togethers, PTA meetings, block parties, neighborhood BBQs, family reunions, toastmasters' clubs...that help you gain confidence and if you still can't overcome the confidence you will be afforded awareness at a minimum.

WHY IS SELF-PROMOTION IMPORTANT?

Self-promotion is about endorsing yourself to others, so you will be considered when future employment and/or advancement opportunities come up. "Luck favors the prepared mind."

Promoting yourself is all part and parcel of job seeking and getting ahead in a company once you land a job. Knowing how to promote yourself requires both skill and natural ability.

 The keys to brand success are self-definition, transparency, authenticity and accountability.
~ Simon Mainwaring

The challenge for all Intrapreneurs is to gain visibility and show strength without seeming to be bragging and coming off as egocentric. This may sound contradictory to the Spartan's Path but the details are the critical element here. We do not advocate the reckless, self-indulgent and shameless promotion of self. Instead we rely on proof in social, dynamic, measurable and demonstrated examples. Take personal credit where credit is due, but shift focus more on sharing the successes of the team and the business milestones with everyone. Thank those that encouraged you, that embraced your idea, close to the point of giving them credit for your idea. Success leverages success. You need to strike just the right balance of promotional strategies that will yield the most effective results and not overdo it! Promote people through sharing your success and they will return the favor in kind.

How people see you in the workplace is critical to your success both in that company and if you seek employment at another place of business down the road. Like an artist gathers his portfolio of his best works, you need to be creating a living picture of you as a successful career holder. Now more than ever it is vital to promote yourself. With the advent of the Internet, social media, and 24/7 businesses, your ability to brand and promote yourself effectively is absolutely essential.

It doesn't matter how skilled you are, how talented you are, or what great ideas you have if no one else knows that. If you hide your light under a bushel, other less deserving, less talented, less creative people will get the opportunities that should have been yours. Why? Because they know how to promote themselves!

Your boss must be able see those skills, talents, and ideas. It's your job to convince your supervisor, your boss, and your colleagues that you are an absolutely invaluable employee. They need to see you as current, knowledgeable, eager, enterprising, resourceful, and a dedicated company person. You need to be the person whose name immediately comes to mind when they think of success. To get ahead you've got to sell yourself. And you need to do it professionally and well!

> Don't worry when you are not recognized, but strive to be worthy of recognition.
> ~ Abraham Lincoln

WAYS TO PROMOTE YOURSELF

1.   Work Proactively on Career Management

In the olden days when an employee was part of the "business family" employees were given in-service training and prepared for the next step on the corporate ladder. Once hired, they were practically assured of moving up that corporate ladder. The company "looked after" them. There was a tacit agreement: You work hard for me and I reward that hard work and loyalty with promotions, raises, incentives. You need only work hard and be loyal.

Employers are no longer looking after an employee's in-service needs. To be ready to move up, an employee needs to manage his own career but more importantly they need to contribute to the evolution.

Employees need to be self-promoting from day one. They need to take control of their own advancement and be prepared with the anticipated skills for their employability and advancement. Managing your career is making sure you have the skills and competencies to perform your present job and the one to which you aspirations.

2. Become the subject matter expert

We are all generalists to a certain extent. In most positions in any business it is rare that you are the only one doing a particular job. You are likely part of a bigger group of people with the same or similar job functions. In the antiquated business model the employee was given a job description and expected to color in the lines. Today the work environment is full of free thinkers; "Millenials", "Gen X'ers and "Baby Boomers" all trying to coexist.

We are seeing the stream widen and in many cases the expectation for promotion is no longer coming from the experienced, loyal employee. These employees are being overlooked by the "hot shot". The one who doesn't swim in the stream, the one who challenges conformity. The ones with such a deep belief in what they do and with a certainty of success that they will push the rules, limits and conformity within their 4 walls. These people are so granular in their knowledge and specialized in one or many areas within their job dynamic that they become nearly irreplaceable. These are the people that will ask for forgiveness instead of permission after the fact, and when they do... they show up with the proof in hand. Sometimes it is met with great accolade and sometimes it is met with punishment but either way, these people understand their value, they will know that in order to receive their output that it will come with their input and at the end of the day it is hard to argue success. When these people are not rewarded or punished they don't see failure in their efforts, they see failure in the company they chose and then they simply move on to a company that will reward and embrace them. This is the change of landscape and it is what successful people and companies already understand and foster.

3. Remember the Rule of One

Remember the Rule of One? All it takes is that one lucky break, knowing that one person, doing the right and being in the right place at the right time. However, the reality is that you've got to kiss a lot of frogs to meet the prince or princess. Be open to all opportunities to promote yourself. You never know when you'll be in the right place at the right time.

4. Create and maintain an online Portfolio

Unless this is your area of expertise, you may have to enlist expert help to get this up and running. First, you need to build a personal portfolio so potential employers can learn more about you, your skills, your talents, and your work. Pages and directions for building a personal landing page are available on such sites as About.Me and Flavors.me. These websites offer excellent, free services to set up an "about me" page on the web. Choose a memorable and easy-to-recall URL. If you have photographic skills you might also built a Flickr portfolio. You could also start your own blog on a WordPress site. Or you can set up a YouTube account.

Your personal portfolio needs a memorable domain name, and a host. At the very least, you need an email address from your own URL, a photo gallery on your site or a blog with your own URL that's full of your ideas and quality articles.

A good start is to look at what others in the field have done to create an online presence.

Just as it is important to create an online presence, it is vital to maintain fresh material on your site. You want to keep visitors returning to check out what's new. If nothing changes, why would they bother to come back? Commit to making changes at least once a week.

5. Make Sure You are Promoting the Best You

Whether online, at a job interview, playing golf with the boss, at a company function, or at a social event, make sure you are promoting your best skills, talents, and traits. If you're trying to promote yourself in a field that you're not skilled, knowledgeable and passionate about this area it will show. If you're not really passionate about what you're doing you need to seek the best skills, talents, ideas, and personality traits you have. Ask yourself: What are my best skills and talents? What am I passionate about? Why am I the best choice for this position? How can I convince others of my passion and skills?

6. Build a Sterling Reputation

Whether you are the CEO, middle management, the mailroom clerk, or an intern, be the best that you can be at what you do and let others know by your work, your attitude and your words. My favorite waitress is one who is unfailingly cheerful, always grabs an opportunity to assist, and clearly loves where she works and what she does. If that girl applies to my business, I will hire her in an instant. She knows how to promote herself!

7. Know and Learn Soft Skills

Anyone can learn hard skills with perseverance, good training, and enough money to purchase good materials and instruction. Hard skills are things like: being able to write a good resume; establishing a website; knowing how to operate the machinery at your business.

Soft skills are just as vital but a lot harder to teach and learn. Soft skills include things like: active listening; empathy; task commitment; team building; enthusiasm; perseverance; respect; honesty; loyalty; optimism; eagerness; task commitment; punctuality and responsibility.

Companies look for soft skills like: leadership, organizational, collegiality, and coaching skills. It's a simple fact: We do business with those we know, like, and trust. Knowing and practicing soft skills is a must when promoting yourself. Employers can teach hard skills. They look for employees who possess the soft skills they desire in their employees.

8. Take Responsibility. Be Accountable

If every employee starts to take ownership of their work,

commits to innovation, learning and discovery and works actively to sell his ideas to management, that business is sure to succeed. How your colleagues and superiors see you is critical to your success. An idea is just a good start.

9. Assess the Skills YOU Need

Learn the skills you need for the job you have—and the next one you want. Be prepared to take on the next challenged by getting training in areas you need. This will show you are eager and it will convince your employer that you know what the job requires and you are anxious to be competent. Technical skills, team work skills and coaching skills are always a plus.

10. Recognize that Your Personal Life is a Factor

With the advent of the Internet, Facebook, YouTube, and smartphones with cameras and immediate access to Facebook and Twitter, your personal life is no longer private. Recognize that your personal life can affect your success in a big way. Even the smallest details of your online presence will be scrutinized. So, too, will the fact that you don't have an online presence! Use it to your advantage. Social media helps you build a positive presence on the Internet.

11. Use Social Media to Network

Your online social networks can help you build a

positive image. You can also use them to "chat" with others who have like interests. Finally, you can use social media networking for learning opportunities.

How do you continuously manage your career?

✓ Keep current on the trends and changes in your career path.

✓ Be a lifelong learner. Take courses, classes, seminars, and workshops to improve your job skills, your technical and communication skills, your teambuilding skills, your presentation skills and your general knowledge.

✓ Keep that resume current and sharp. It doesn't matter whether you are job searching. Update your resume every time you learn a new skill or take a new course.

✓ In this day of sophisticated business software, there is no excuse for not having a well-organized and continuously changing contacts list. Keep it current and make sure to touch with your contacts regularly.

✓ Social networking sites, such as LinkedIn, Facebook, and Twitter are great tools for keeping up with contacts and what is going on in your business sector. If you don't know how to do this, take a course, attend a workshop or seek out a mentor. Don't forget what a resource kids are in this area!

✓ Think about using the expertise of an employability coach or resources such as your area Human Resources Development

✓ Look after yourself. It is important to your stamina, your attitude, your self-confidence and your image to remain healthy. Eat right. Get enough sleep. Exercise. Keep active. Don't become an all-work-and-no-play person.
✓ Find ways to manage stress with exercise, rest, diet, and hobbies.

✓ Remain open to advice and strategies for managing your career and improving your skills.

BUILDING YOUR ARMY

The Spartans understood the power on an army better than anyone of their time and likely since. There is much known about the riggers and training of the Spartan warrior bur what is often less talked about is the supporting team. In Sparta the women played a major role in the team. The women had as much of a regimen as the men did. They went through their own form of training which included running, wrestling and exercising. They were also trained in hand to hand combat and weapons training. While the women were never meant to see a battle field it was the goal of the entire civilization to protect Sparta and when the warriors were away, there would never be a threat that this acropolis without walls would ever be fortified be another army.

The modern day Spartan in business is an Intrapreneur. This Spartan understands the need for teamwork and the depth of team just like that of the Spartans past. The

Intrapreneur is a master of his or her craft but they are also quite masterful at networking. In leadership they will tend to defer credit to those that helped them and take none for themselves. Much like the Spartan they are selfless with an understanding of building up a loyal army. This will not only give you strength in numbers, create an invaluable and audible voice but it will also give the members of your army an opportunity to continually get better. You see as the general collaborates with the army, the individuals in the army bring equal but separate strengths to the table until an environment of student teacher is ubiquitous amongst all.

 It doesn't matter how good you are, and believe me you are good, but you can't do everything.
~ Greg Otterbein

WITH A LITTLE HELP FROM MY FRIENDS

You don't have to do self-promotion as a solo. Many people shy away from self-promotion fearing that others will see them as a blow hard, a wind bag, a Narcissus, or just plain arrogant. They could easily sing their own praise to their colleagues or their boss but they are shy about "tooting their own horn" and they are humble and practical whenever the praise is given. They are the first to recognize those around them instead.

A Spartan will not do the promoting of oneself directly. Here are some ways to get help from friends, acquaintances, colleagues, employers, cyber friends, and clients.

1. Get Your Clients and Buyers to Sell for You

Showcase testimonials sought from previous clients, colleagues, and employers.

Testimonials add credibility. People trust the experiences of others like themselves. Place these testimonials in your portfolio and on your website. Ask for a testimonial after clients have used your services or products. Make it easy by asking two key questions such as:

- How has this product or person helped you?

- What was the best thing about working with it/them?

2. Do a Little Each Day

Send a few tweets, some emails, a Facebook comment or a promotion of a new product or service out each day. This maintains contact with previous clients and your peer group. Make it a regular habit and always be authentic. It builds trust, familiarity, and a positive link.

3. Consider Craigslist

This is a good opportunity to access new clients, announce a new product or service or search the jobs section of the site. Get into the habit of asking people if they can be added to your newsletter so that they are updated in future of your work. Craigslist will advertise your services in the classified areas for service providers.

4. Build Google Circles

Google's latest social media concept is Google +. It is really useful for promoting yourself in business, friends, family or other "Circles". You can organize people within groups to share and see things. This allows you to keep track of particular groups, such as: clients, colleagues, prospects and keep them separate from more personal contacts. This is a great time saver when you wish to send out information or request testimonials or your promotional campaigns. With Google + you can even share progress reports.

5. Use Facebook Likes

Ask friends, family, colleagues, and cyber friends to 'like' your Facebook page. Companies like Coke and Diesel have offered discounts to attract 'likes'. This gains attention for your page—effectively promoting you to all the friends of friends. Consider an incentive like a newsletter subscription, an e-Book, or blog membership.

6. Capitalize on Friends' Creative Talents

A great way to provide promotion is to use photographs, videos, guest articles, and blogs about you. If you have creative friends enlist their resources to create a slide show, a photo collage, Facebook photo album, or a video or writing articles or blogs documenting your work space, lifestyle, work process, activities, hobbies. People find this interesting. This builds trust in you and your products and services. It adds a vital human element to information about you that people can see for themselves. It also attracts people to your website.

7. Share your Expertise for FREE!

People with credibility in any area from creating éclairs to choosing high-return investments can share their expertise to build a following, promote themselves, save having to answer the same question multiple times. Through YouTube or a video on Facebook or on their blog, they can share what they are good at. Good examples include: designer Stefan Sagmeister, Twitter creator Jack Dorsey and the chef Jamie Oliver. Sharing what you do well will build an audience, increase your credibility and build a reputation.

8. Tell a Story

People like Richard Branson, Dolly Parton and Steve Jobs know how to tell a story. People are drawn to these stories like how Branson developed Virgin Airlines or how Dolly Parton came to write "Coat of Many Colors". These stories drive people to their websites and increase product sales. Use a story or a dialogue or an interview with a friend to paint a picture of who you are. This makes you more memorable and builds your credibility without your seeming to be bragging.

Cabbage Patch Dolls each come with a story about the manufacturer and the product.

9.   Promote Yourself through Quora Q&A

Quora, a social question and answer site, is popular amongst techies, entrepreneurs, and Intrapreneurs. It is a great way to get advice on a wide range of issues and products. This is a great spot to get good quality, first-hand advice from people. It is also an excellent place to promote yourself and your area of expertise. It often generates client following. Again this does not feel or sound like bragging, crowing or stealing the limelight.

10.   Try a Gravatar to Increase Visibility

'Globally Recognized Avatar' is the small photo or image that appears next to a comment left on blogs. It's important that you have a Gravatar if you make use of blog commenting for self-promotion and online networking. Having one is part of creating an image of yourself that is trustworthy, part of building a personal brand, and important in building relationships in the process. Having an image also means people are more likely to attract clicks over to your site, when a comment is left.

11.   Say it in a Poster

Create a poster or leaflet that includes all the key stuff about you and your services. Include a picture of your recent work. Enlist really creative friends to help you do this in an interesting way. People will remember you, your work and what you do.

12. Use LinkedIn to Create a Mailing List

LinkedIn is a practical and easy resource to search for and connect with other creative professionals.

Lastly, remember the Spartan vision. Everyone is an equal, everyone has a job to do and a function that contributes to the State. You must give as well as you receive and treat every single person you meet with equality, dignity and respect regardless of position, status or affiliation. Anyone stands to learn and benefit from everyone.

 Unity is strength... when there is teamwork and collaboration, wonderful things can be achieved.
~ Mattie Stepanek

The last rule in the new workplace is also counter to Legacy. The legacy is looking for the winning idea. This is futile. A singular winning idea creates contempt and lack of depth. The single winning idea creates downfall, hostility and meritocracy.

The Spartan Intrepreneur understands that in today's changing work environment collaboration is the winner of the day. The best ideas are combined, modified from their original form and the idea always ends up becoming bigger that its creator because the creator is no one and everyone. It is magnanimous and oblivious. It is bigger than all of us and more effective than one of us.

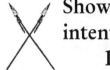 **Show your total talent daily and be very intentional!!**
Dan Carroll

BUSINESS LANDMINES

The Modern Day Spartan has learned from the past the importance of the battle and the war and the difference between tactic and strategy.

Better to lose the battle and win the war.

Tactics are the devices used in the battle; strategies are the plans that win the wars.

The Spartan Intrapreneur knows what mountains are worth dying on and will fight for their beliefs and the beliefs of their team without peril or fear a reprisal. The Spartan Intrapreneur knows it is in their company's best interest to have them on their team as opposed to the team of their rival and in that confidence they know they are an employee, friend or family member that brings great value to the table and if that value is scoffed at, then they are at the wrong table and the Spartan Intrapreneur will not hesitate to find a new table. What's worse, they will bring their army with them.

While all of this sounds nice you must again remember the difference between the battle and the war. The tactic is to win; the strategy is to never be defeated by one person.

Business landmines usually exist in the Legacy Minded. These are usually one-offs but they can be a group. Sometimes you can work with them, sometimes around them and sometimes you must work through them. The idea of changing the mind of a legacy can be futile. A legacy likes proof, demands proof and will be the first to say the proof is anomalous or a one off. The legacy will require multiple data sets, proof after proof after proof. Hoping to either wear out the Intrepreneur or poke holes in their ideas as this threatens everything the legacy has ever known and thus makes them vulnerable and tenable. To the legacy this is not a matter of will. Dinosaurs had will and could not be budged. Sometimes the only way around a Legacy is to get a buy in from another source.

The key strategy to overcoming legacy is the Sandwich Effect. The filling representing the Legacy and each slice of bread your constituency. You must build a team of support from the bottom up and the top down in order to smash the legacy and make them uncomfortable. Eventually the filling will either stick to both sides of the bread or ooze out of the side. Either way they will yield when you build!

The Spartan Intrepreneur is no stranger to adversity in the work place. No stranger to having to prove themselves over and over. Just like the Spartan warriors your legacy is never finished after just one battle and the war will rage on as long as your beliefs challenge someone else's.

Identifying the corporate landmines are one thing, avoiding them forever is impossible so the real meat on the bone comes from being able to manage and overcome them.

The premise is really one as old as time. The majority of things that will stand in your way will be party to one of two things. You are either a threat to yourself or to someone else. The best way to avoid the first to understand what you are doing. More important that the understanding of what you are doing is to understand the impact it will have on others. From there you must understand the implications it can have throughout. Now this is where it gets tricky. A Spartan Intrapreneur understands the importance of an advisory board. Through collaboration and the path of the Spartan you will achieve great things in collaboration and helping others. While the advisory board may not be formal, the idea of having people with areas of expertise and knowledge in which is unique to them yet they are willing to share because they understand your motivation and passion for doing the right thing. This asset will prove itself your most valuable form of currency in any business. And too it is always good to give as well as you receive. You have to be somebody's advisor as well. Again, it does you no good to be echo or a sounding board, but a person of integrity and class when it comes to giving it to people straight.

Having a plan that is bullet proof is also the way of the Spartan Intrapreneur. Quite simply put, we have all had ideas shot down. Not learning from those angles in which the bullets were able to break through compels history to repeat itself and in order to make your ideas and strategies bullet proof you have to predict the angles and motivations against the best laid plan. See the whole picture, get support and feedback and be prepared to be told no 100 times. At the end of the day, working through the minefield you will understand the value of having a team of supports surrounding you at your rear, in front and at your flank. Pressure from all angles and support from a legion of fans or an army of likeminded people will create so much pressure that any bad objection will either get squeezed out or forced to concede.

Another technique in handling corporate landmines comes in the form of deflecting the wins onto the loser. Using this technique to promote the person opposed to the idea will often win out the day and potentially make the path free of resistance in the future.

For example when someone shoots down your idea but you still move forward with it, you give the credit to that person for forcing you to make it better and because of them and the pressure and objections they forced you to think of and plan for, the goal was accomplished.

At the end of the day there will simply be people with a different ideology and there will be some people whose minds you will not be able to change, no matter how good you become, no matter how strong your track record. We have all dealt with people like this along our careers and the only way to win in this situation is to choose to not even ignore them.

"Chose not to even ignore them." ~ Dan Carroll

This quote is pretty profound and it impacted me in a very clear way. I know I was guilty of this in the past. I would spend too much time worrying about what that person thought or how I could get them to agree with me or eventually win them over and at the end of the day all that did was validate their power and put me in a submissive position affording them a position they likely didn't earn or deserve.

THE CHANGING LANDSCAPE

Some Final Thoughts...

We shy away from self-promotion because we don't want to appear full of ourselves or puffed up. In truth that is self-adulation or self-aggrandizement. Self-promotion is putting our best self out there honestly and in a forthright manner. Allowing promotion or recognition and creating a path of inclusion, team winning and success is nothing to be ashamed of.

For example if a writer refers to himself as a "bestselling" author, that is self-promotion. If he says he's "the best writer north of the Mason Dixon Line" that is self-adulation. Self-promotion is "putting yourself out there". It involves sharing ideas, concepts, and a vision. Self-aggrandizement is just bragging about your accomplishments or your possessions. Sharing your ideas, concepts, and ideals inspires hope. Bragging just turns people off. As Nathan Hangden author of Beyond Blogging points out: "There are fans out there for every self-promoter. Your task is to find them... that, and to make it easy for them to bring a friend."

Bigger than promotion is relevance. In our changing landscape and the evolution of business it is nearly impossible to keep up. In story after story there are examples of companies that had been in business for over a century, half a century and even a quarter and at an alarming rate, these businesses are falling off the face of the planet.

Case study after case study keeps pointing back to one thing, they didn't stay relevant. They found that keeping up was harder than quitting or giving up. The fight to get there is sometimes so hard that and when that fight to get there produced a favorable result for many years it is easy to confuse yesterday's success with tomorrow assumption. This is the point where those ugly legacy rules kick in. Well this is how we have always done it to be successful so this is how we are always going to do it.

Understand people fear what they don't understand. We reject what scares us. In general the motivation to succeed is trumped by the fear of failure. We would rather do nothing and be safe than take a risk and fail. No matter how great the risk versus reward ratio stacks up and sometimes without a known risk at all, we will still tend to err on the side of caution. What that means is we are not prepared. We err on the side of caution as we fear the side of progression. This story has now been written the data has been captured. This idea is dead. In an earlier chapter we had mentioned that all organic things reach a point at which they stop growing and when that point is reached that is when these things begin to die.

You will one day be the legacy, the dinosaur, the bad idea. Be mindful of what you knew and always be open to what others can provide.

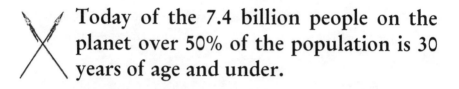 **Today of the 7.4 billion people on the planet over 50% of the population is 30 years of age and under.**

The generation behind you will be able to scale faster, multitask better, comprehend more, communicate more, experience more in a lower impact environment and their ideas will be better, faster, more measurable and more technologically developed. You will have to decide if you will lay down your sword and go the way of the Spartans. If you will become extinct or if you will capture your history, continue to strive for self-improvement or will you think you have nothing left to learn, believe you will always be able to learn something from everyone or only think they should be learning from you.

Remember the Spartan's Code for once you are a Spartan you are a Spartan until you die and even in death your legacy will live on because you moved mountains, overcame the odds and did the unexpected to great ends.

THE SPARTAN CODE

The Spartan is on a quest for freedom. Freedom of money, freedom of time and freedom of purpose. The Spartan is not selfish with their ideas; when they learn, they share. A Spartan understands the value of collaboration and is not interested in making themselves stronger without making the entire team stronger. A Spartan finds likeminded people that fight for faith, family and purpose. In a world where ideals have become unpopular the Spartan will win out the day.

The Spartan will pick their battles wisely and know what mountains are worth dying on. The Spartan understands sacrifice and knows we occasionally have to lose the battle to win the war. We are balanced, deliberate and authentic. There is not one of us amongst the best of us better than the rest of us.

THAX TURNER

Does your history, your backstory, and your family legacy define you? Does it propel your success or limit your achievements?

My name is Thax Turner, and long ago I made the conscious decision that my past would not determine my future, and that my potential was worth going to battle for. See, I didn't grow up with the privilege of wealth. But one day, as a boy, my grandmother (a very wise woman) gave me a bit of advice. And that advice helped to shape every decision I made from then on out.

She said, "Thax, never let failure stop you. Failure is just a measure of how badly a person desires something."

And I realized then, that if I were to just try to "think" my goals into realization, I'd never get anywhere. True desire, dreams worth realizing, would in of itself, compel me to complete any mission.

I left home at seventeen to join the US Army, and, doing what was expected of me, I went to college after my discharge. Soon, I joined the ranks of corporate America, thus initiating a professional career.

I failed. Often. But I always failed forward! Learning from where I went wrong in both work opportunities and personal relationships. Remembering what my grandmother had taught me, I accepted each failure as a lesson and I strived to learn from each one of them.

Staying the course hasn't been easy, it never is. Since the early days of my career I've achieved numerous promotions and racked up significant salary increases. I've earned by blood, sweat, and tears, every rung I've climbed up that ladder. God gives us the ability to achieve our goals but it's up to us to make them happen. I believe in a life of unlimited potential and our choice is to take that chance or ignore it.

My grandmother's advice was a catalyst for me and the greatest lesson I've learned is that I can accept failure, without giving in to defeat. I don't give up. I seek out solutions in the midst of despair. I keep my vision, my goals, and my higher purpose in sight. I help and support others who have the same drive and desire to elevate their lives and position. It is with this passion, my spirit of true collaboration and willingness to give that we wrote this book.

They say that life's challenges are nothing but diversions along the great journey. Given the right tools, your pursuit of success will become habitual. I'm a living testament to this. We never stop learning, growing, achieving! In faith, in family and in our work, I toast to your success and wish you the wisdom and courage it will take to realize the life of a Modern Day Spartan.

May we fight the good fight together!

Thax

TheModernDaySpartan.com

ABOUT THE AUTHORS

Ronald "Bo" Bryant

As a kid from a single family home I was always encouraged from my mother to seek and explore what fascinated me. I had no restrictions in the sense of my own development. Like most mothers, mine told me I could do and become anything in the world that I wanted to do or become. Some mothers and fathers merely tell that to their children, but my mother expected it and demanded it.

My father taught me to always challenge both the status quo and the rules. He warned of the perils of intellectual slavery and the importance of free thought, free enterprise and going my own direction. My most memorable quote from my father was this...**"Give a boy a hammer and the world is his nail."**

I have never been accused of swimming in the stream but I have certainly been asked to. Growing up with little means and unconventional learning, coupled with tremendous faith, support and people who believed in me, it paved a road that would later be called the Spartan's Path.

I have built a career on being focused on how things work. How can things be better, work better, return better. How can the goals of a company align with the goals of a customer. How can the voice of the customer be heard and more importantly how can you get a company to understand the importance of what the customer wants and how to make that voice align with the needs of a company.

Often times I have had to create a ripple, I have upset some people and made others very happy. In the end I have done what I do because I believe in what I do.

Like Thax, I have owned a number of companies, been an entrepreneur and an Intrapreneur. I have written business plans and charters and I have written bestselling books. I have developed my own career path through my companies and through the companies I have been blessed to work with.

The most important key to our collective success has been our constitution, beliefs, integrity, conviction, balance, family and collaboration. This has been a hard fought path but one of much fulfillment and we welcome you and encourage you to embrace your authenticity, your eccentricity and your passion to join us on this journey to impact your life and the lives of those around you!

Stop being who you are and start being who you want to become!

Ron

TheModernDaySpartan.com

Wanna dive deeper, go to
www.TheModernDaySpartan.com and receive
our free blueprint on the Spartan's Path.
Start you path to becomes the best version of
yourself right now!

Check out our weekly show on
blogtalkradio.com/TheModernSpartan

**Go to The Modern Day Spartan on Facebook
and chat with the authors and ask us
questions!**

Contact us at Go@TheSpartansPath.com

13236935R00090

Made in the USA
San Bernardino, CA
14 July 2014